QUEEN BEE

SUZY K QUINN

This book is for any girl who has had trouble with friends at school. Who are you in this story? And who do you want to be?

PART 1

THE EMERGING QUEEN

'A colony of honeybees has only one queen. If there is more than one, the queens will fight to the death.

SCARLETT

THIS IS what pupils are supposed to wear at St Valentine's School for Girls:

Navy blazer with St Valentine's logo
Navy skirt (must cover the knee)
Black leather lace-up shoes (no sports shoes, Velcro or heels)
Stiff-collared shirt and tie
Hair must be tied back in a navy hairband.

I should have worn school uniform on my first day, of course, but it didn't arrive on time. So I ended up wearing one of my big sister's skirt suits. I'm tall for my age, so the suit was short in some places, baggy in others. My hair sat in a frizzy, red cloud around my shoulders, having fought against three hair elastics and won. In short, I stood out. And not in a good way.

When I arrived at the school gates, I smiled and waved as girls walked past. They all stared at me, open-mouthed.

The St Valentine's girls wore perfect, navy uniforms with shiny black shoes. Their school bags matched. Their hairbands matched. Their gleaming ponytails swung as they walked. It was so different to my New York school, where boys and girls turned up in their own clothes, shouting, laughing and racing along on scooters.

'Hi!' I kept smiling, but no one smiled back. One group of girls looked me up and down, then walked away whispering and giggling. That felt horrible. Still, I held my head high as I walked through the gates, trying to look friendly.

As I reached the school, a woman came charging towards me through the main doors. She was short and sort of shrivelled looking. And angry.

'Who are you?' The woman flapped her hands like she was trying to put out a fire. 'What are you doing here?'

'I'm the new girl,' I said. 'Scarlett King. Will you be my new teacher –'

'I'm not a teacher,' snapped the woman. 'I'm Mrs Brawn. The office manager. And I can't possibly let you into school dressed like this.'

'I'm sorry,' I said. 'My school uniform didn't arrive on time. It should be here by tomorrow –'

'Are you American?' asked Mrs Brawn.

'No, I'm British,' I said. 'But we lived in New York for five years so I've picked up the accent.' I gave a little laugh. 'You know, it's funny. In the US, they thought I sounded British. But here, everyone thinks I'm American.'

Mrs Brawn didn't smile. 'You can't wear those clothes here. Miss Miel won't allow it.'

'Miss Miel is the headmistress, isn't she?' I smiled. 'I've heard all about her. She used to be a ballerina for the Royal Ballet. I love dancing. I can't wait to meet –'

'I'll find you something from lost property,' Mrs Brawn interrupted. 'Come this way.'

Mrs Brawn led me through a warren of corridors, and into a cloakroom lined with neat navy coats. She pulled a plastic box of stained clothes from a shelf and rummaged inside.

'You're very tall,' said Mrs Brawn. 'And thin. I'm not sure anything in here will fit. We need to make sure your knees are covered.' She handed me a huge navy skirt, then frowned at my messy red hair. 'Now what can we do about your hair? It isn't tied back.'

'It's really hard to tie back,' I admitted. 'There's so much of it. Most hair elastics snap.'

Mrs Brawn frowned. 'Yes. Well, put this skirt on at least.'

The skirt was five times too big around the waist, so I took a spare school tie from the box and used it as a belt. I giggled when I looked in the mirror. It looked so silly, but Mrs Brawn didn't see the funny side.

'Come with me.' Mrs Brawn marched me along more corridors. 'We take school seriously here. You're not a child anymore.' Eventually, she stopped outside a classroom. 'You will behave like a young lady. Do you understand? Fun and games are over.'

I gave a rapid nod.

Mrs Brawn turned to the classroom door. 'This is your form room. In America, you would call this a homeroom. But here, it is a form room, and Mrs Singh is your form teacher. You must come here every morning for registration. Do you understand?'

I nodded again.

Mrs Brawn opened the classroom door and called inside: 'Mrs Singh? I have the new girl for you. I found her wandering around the playground in non-school uniform. She's still wearing *boots*, I'm sad to say. But I've smartened her up the best I can. She's American.'

Dozens of faces turned to stare at the classroom doorway. Mrs Brawn moved out of the way to expose me in my loose skirt.

'Welcome, Scarlett.' Mrs Singh gave me a warm smile, dimples appearing in her chubby brown cheeks. She wore the kind of stretchy, comfortable clothing you buy with your groceries and had a loose ponytail glittering with grey sparkles.

'Hi.' I smiled and waved.

'I'll be your form tutor, Scarlett,' said Mrs Singh. 'I teach personal and social education and I'm also school counsellor. As you can see by my classroom.' She gestured to posters about feelings and emotions on the walls. 'And if you ever want to talk to someone, I have a private office right outside.'

'Thanks so much, Mrs Singh,' I said. 'I'm so grateful to be here. I mean, it's totally different to my school in New York, but I'll try –'

'Are you American?' Mrs Singh asked.

'Um, no.' I heard the door slam behind me. 'My family are from London, but we lived in New York so I have a teeny bit of an accent.'

'Girls!' Mrs Singh turned to the class. 'Are we going to make Scarlett feel welcome?'

'Yes, Mrs Singh,' the girls chanted.

'Wonderful,' said Mrs Singh. 'Now, where should I sit you?' She looked around the class. Her eyes fell on a short, perfectly groomed girl, with a pointy face and shiny brown hair.

'Lottie?'

'Yes, Mrs Singh?' the girl trilled.

'You'll look after Scarlett, won't you?'

I gave Lottie a hopeful smile.

Lottie looked at me. Really looked at me, her sharp, blue eyes taking in my messy hair and saggy skirt. She nudged the large, blonde girl beside her, and they both giggled.

Then Lottie sat up extra straight, cleared her throat like she was making a speech and said:

'Actually, Mrs Singh, I'm quite busy with the dance

competition right now. So maybe it's better if someone else looks after the new girl.'

Mrs Singh frowned. 'But really Lottie, you're our lower-school head girl –'

A hand shot up at the back of the class.

'I'll look after Scarlett,' said a cheerful girl with a long, black fishtail braid.

'Thank you, Amina,' said Mrs Singh.

'Yes, thank you so much.' I gave the girl a warm smile.

Amina smiled back, showing very white teeth in dark brown skin. There was a crossword puzzle on her desk and a pen shaped like a feather.

I headed towards her desk.

'You're a life saver,' I whispered. 'I thought I might end up standing for the whole of registration.'

'No trouble,' said Amina. 'I know what it's like to be new. This is my friend, Marianne.' She pointed to a pale girl sitting beside her.

'Do you play chess?' Marianne asked, blinking clear blue eyes at me.

'No,' I admitted. 'But I'm sure I could learn.'

'Give Scarlett a chance to sit down, Marianne,' said Amina. 'Save the chess talk for break time.'

'It's fine.' I gave Marianne my best smile. 'I don't mind. At least someone is talking to me.'

'Yes, some girls here aren't very friendly,' said Marianne, in a high, warbly voice. 'Lottie and her friends can be unkind.'

'Yes.' I glanced at Lottie, who was whispering to her blonde friend. 'I noticed.'

. . .

After registration, I was taken to an empty classroom to complete maths and English tests. Then the bell rang for break time, and I was sent into the playground with the other girls.

That's the worst part of starting a new school – break and lunchtime. At first, you have no one to hang out with.

I wandered around the school grounds, trying to find Amina and Marianne. Then I stumbled across a dance studio. It was right behind the science block, doors wide open, with a ballet barre, mirrors and shiny rubber floor.

Some girls were inside the studio, practising a dance routine.

As I came closer, I saw one of the girls was Lottie.

'Hey!' I waved from the doorway. 'Wow, this studio is so cool. I'm glad I found this place. I love dancing. Can I join you?'

All the girls stared at me. The large, blonde girl beside Lottie said: 'You're the new girl, right? Your family moved into that massive house at the end of our street.'

'Err ... I guess.' I blushed.

'My dad sold your family that house,' said the girl. 'He works in property. You have a swimming pool, right?'

'Oh, I wouldn't call it a pool right now,' I laughed. 'More like a hole in the ground with blue tiles. Hey, I wondered. Could I dance with you guys?'

'Sorry,' said Lottie. 'Our group is full. We're practising for a very important dance contest.'

'That sounds awesome.' I gave a good-natured smile. 'I love dance contests. I entered tons of them back in New York. I never won anything, but I loved the experience. Hey, do you think there might be other girls here who might want to dance with me?'

'No one else in the lower school dances,' said Lottie,

fixing me with hard, blue eyes. 'Just us. Look, can you just go away?'

I stood there for a moment, not quite knowing what to say.

'Um ... okay,' I heard myself say. 'No big deal.'

As I wandered away, Amina came hurrying over. 'Scarlett! There you are. We've been looking for you everywhere.'

'Thank goodness,' I said. 'A friendly face. What happened to the head girl at this school? Does she drink unfriendly tea or something?'

'Lottie has her favourite friends,' said Amina. 'That's just how she is. Marianne and I thought you might want to play chess. We have our own travel set.'

'Sure,' I smiled. 'That sounds great. I have to warn you, though. I really don't know how to play. Hey, I don't suppose you girls are into dancing at all?'

Amina shook her head. 'No. Only Lottie and those girls are into dancing.'

'Right.' I nodded. 'Okay. Let's go play chess.'

All in all, my first day at St Valentine's School was not fun. Why can't we just go back to New York? I had LOADS of friends in New York. I miss them so much.

LOTTIE

My nickname at school is Little Miss Perfect. Which is funny, because my life is far from perfect.

My parents go to marriage therapy, I need a tutor to help with mathematics and I'm really short for my age. Also, I have bad eyesight and it's getting worse.

Everyone *thinks* I'm perfect because I work really, really hard. I do extra schoolwork every evening, dance training at break times and Dad makes word games to help my vocabulary.

This year, I've already won the school swimming gala, a short story competition and an English award. Oh, and Miss Miel made me head girl.

I'm always top of the class, but only because I put in lots of extra work. I want to be the best. Winning is important to me. I come from a very competitive family.

My big sister wins *everything*, but it's easier for her. She's naturally clever and sporty. No one ever thinks Cassandra and I are sisters. Cassandra is tall, blonde and athletic, whereas I'm small and brown-haired with a pointy face and thin lips.

Maybe having Cassandra as a sister makes me more competitive. I don't know. All I know is, I don't feel that great about myself most of the time and winning makes me feel better.

Some people say I'm competitive about friendships too, but I don't think that's true.

Here's the way I look at things.

Some people are A people, and some are B people. That's not me being mean. It's just how things are. You can't be friends with everybody.

I'm not saying the A people are better than the B people. I'm just saying, you can only have so many important people in your life.

Farrah, Primrose and Sophie are my A people.

Farrah moved to Hiverstock three years ago and we just totally hit it off. She's my very best friend. My number one. Farrah is tall and blonde, like my sister, and really funny.

I've known Primrose and Sophie since nursery. We didn't hang out as much until Farrah moved here, but now the four of us are always together.

Primrose has reddish-brown hair, which is nearly chin-length now. She used to have short hair, like a boy, and wear baseball caps and oversized hoodies. But since Farrah came along, Primrose wears ballet shoes and tight jeans like the rest of us and is growing her hair. I think because she's sick of Farrah teasing her.

Sophie – how do I describe Sophie? She looks like a princess, with bright blue eyes and the longest brown, curly hair. She has amazing clothes and is always so well turned out. Just perfect. And she's really sweet and kind. I can't imagine her falling out with anyone.

So they're my A girls. The ones I picked for my dance squad and invite to cinema dates and sleepovers. We spend every break and lunch together and go to the pizza park every weekend.

The pizza park is just the local park, but there are food places by the lake.

I suppose the park could just as easily be called the baked potato park or the hot sausage park. But since we all love the wood-fired pizza, we call it the pizza park.

In the summer, Farrah, Primrose, Sophie and I get pizza every Saturday and practise our dancing by the lake. There's a big dance contest coming up, and we need every spare moment. Sometimes the girls moan about practising so much, but they understand we need to put in the time.

Then there are B people. The girls I invite to birthday parties and play sports with and that kind of thing. I like them, but they're not part of my inner circle.

Everyone else – I don't really notice.

Actually, that's not true. I did notice someone today. The new girl, Scarlett King. Oh my god, *what* a show-off.

Of course, we'd all heard about Scarlett before she

started school because her family bought the biggest house in the village.

Four Chimneys has seven bedrooms, a swimming pool, a garden kitchen and its own woodlands. Farrah's dad told us all about it because he was the agent who sold it to Scarlett's family.

'That family must be doing well for themselves,' he said.

Full of themselves, more like.

Scarlett asked to join *my* dance squad today. I mean, who does she think she is? Just because she has a big house doesn't mean she can just push her way in.

I was like, no, sorry. See you later.

Maybe it was a little unfriendly, but honestly, I have so many things on my mind right now – what with my optician's appointment and the dance contest and everything.

Every year, the Dolores Rush Dance Academy holds a contest to find 'exceptional dance talent'. Usually, only dance schools can enter, but Miss Miel knows Dolores Rush personally, so our school enters too.

Miss Miel chooses my squad every year for the contest. We haven't won yet, but we have a great routine this year and the girls are working hard on their fitness. No one works as hard as me, of course, but they're getting there.

Dance contest winners get huge cash prizes, so it's a big deal. The best solo act also receives a scholarship to the Dolores Rush Dance Academy, but I'm not interested in moving schools. Nor are Farrah, Primrose or Sophie. We're happy enough to win the money and stay at St Valentine's.

SCARLETT

My St Valentine's uniform arrived last night, so I'd hoped to fit in a little better today. Everyone still stared when I came into registration, though – I think because of my height and my hair. Oh, and Lottie whispered to her friends, smirked and looked in my direction. Then they all laughed. I ignored them and sat with Amina and Marianne.

'Hey, do you know anything about a dance contest?' I asked, taking a seat. 'Lottie mentioned it yesterday.'

'Oh, you mean the Dolores Rush Dance Contest,' said Amina. 'It's a big thing. Miss Miel enters one dance squad from our school every year. And it's always Lottie's dance squad.'

'Dolores *Rush*?' I said. 'Isn't she retired?'

'She's retired from dancing,' said Amina. 'But she runs a dance school in London. Every year she holds a contest, and there are very big prizes to be won. The best solo dancer wins a hundred thousand pounds and a scholarship to Dolores's dance academy. It's a very big deal.'

'That's amazing,' I said. 'Can I enter?'

'Technically, yes,' said Marianne, lifting her head from a crossword puzzle. 'Any girl in this school can enter. But save your precious time for your schoolwork. Miss Miel always chooses Lottie's dance squad.'

'How come?' I asked

'Because Lottie is lower-school head girl and Miss Miel loves her,' said Marianne. 'It's not fair, but school isn't a democracy. None of our teachers are elected.'

'But if I wanted to enter,' I probed, 'I could?'

'I believe there's still time,' said Marianne. 'Miss Miel usually makes her decision a few weeks before the contest. But you need a dance squad.'

'A squad?' I said. 'I thought you said there was a solo prize?'

'The solo prize goes to a dancer within a winning squad,' Amina explained. 'But no one will make a squad with you if you're going against Lottie.'

'Why not?' I asked.

'Because Lottie is a queen bee,' said Amina.

'What's a queen bee?' I asked.

'It's a metaphor,' said Marianne. 'For a girl who's in charge of everyone. Queen bees are extremely interesting creatures. They're given the best food, while the other female bees do all the work, collecting the nectar and so on. The whole hive revolves around them. And when new queen bees are born, they fight to the death for control of the hive.'

'Maybe you could ask Lottie if she has room for you on her squad,' Amina suggested. 'If you're a good dancer, she might say yes.'

'I already asked to dance with Lottie,' I said. 'She told me to get lost.'

Marianne sucked in her breath. 'That's extremely rude. But don't take it personally. Lottie is rude to most people. At least she said something to you. She doesn't talk to me at all.'

That evening, I pleaded with Mum and Jamie to put me in a new school.

Jamie is Mum's boyfriend and my sort of stepdad. He is ten years older than Mum, but has bleached blond hair and bright red glasses, like a hip twenty-something. Jamie is from New York originally, and we never thought he'd move to the UK with us. But I guess he loves Mum more than we thought.

'Please, Mum,' I begged. 'Can't you at least send me to a school where there are boys as well?'

Mum tipped take-out spaghetti onto plates, being very careful not to get carbonara sauce on her green, silk dress. My mum is the kind of woman who looks magazine perfect all the time. Her fingernails always match her outfit, and her shiny black hair lies flat all day.

'You're not moving schools, Scarlett,' said Mum, sprinkling a plastic pot of parmesan over the spaghetti. 'The arrangements have already been made.'

'Please,' I begged. 'St Valentine's is so unfriendly. Only two girls are nice to me, but neither of them dance. I need some dance buddies.'

'Maybe you should talk to your sister,' said Mum. 'She'll give you better advice than I can, darling. It's been years since I was at school.'

My big sister, Zara, moved from New York to England with us, but studies in London. Mum says Zara will visit soon, but I'm not so sure. Zara avoids being at home whenever she can.

When I was younger, I used to look up to Zara and wish we could be better friends. But these days, I just see her as this alien twenty-year-old with big, green cat eyes and shiny, black hair. We have different fathers, and it shows in our looks and personalities.

I'm all out there, whereas Zara is more reserved, like Mum. But she's not *like* Mum, if you know what I mean. Zara is nice, deep down.

'You had a ton of friends in New York,' said Jamie, forking up spaghetti. 'You'll make friends in no time. Hey, how about the real estate guy who sold us this house?' Jamie turned to Mum. 'He has a daughter in Scarlett's class. Why don't we invite them over for a barbecue?'

'What's the daughter's name?' I asked.

'Farrah,' said Jamie.

'*Farrah*,' I said. 'No way. She's one of the really unfriendly ones. She's best friends with the head girl.'

'Kids are always unfriendly at first,' said Jamie. 'You have to break through.'

'Please don't invite the Turners to our house.' Mum wrapped spaghetti around her fork. 'Kelly Turner already sends me twenty WhatsApp messages a day. I don't want to encourage her.'

'I don't want them to come either,' I said. 'I just want to go back to New York.'

Then I started crying.

'For God's sake, Scarlett,' said Mum. 'You have your own bathroom here and a walk-in wardrobe of clothes. You even have a swimming pool. Why can't you be grateful?'

'No one can swim in the pool,' I snivelled. 'It needs to be cleaned –'

'I've lost my appetite.' Mum stood up, slender and elegant as always. 'Honestly, Scarlett. If you think school is bad, wait until you join the real world.' With that, she glided off upstairs with her glass of wine.

'Chin up, kid,' said Jamie, grabbing his plate of spaghetti and following Mum out of the kitchen. 'It'll get better.'

I sat in the kitchen alone for a while, feeling utterly wretched. For a moment, I thought about calling Dad. Maybe I could beg to move into his New York apartment. But ... no. Dad isn't a reliable parent. Anyway, he hardly ever picks up the phone.

LOTTIE

Today was the worst day of my life.

Mum took me to the opticians after school, and it happened. The thing I've been dreading.

Mr Samuels, the optician, said I have to wear glasses all the time. Really horrible, super ugly glasses that make me look like my dad. I'm not allowed contact lenses because I have dry eyes and something called astigmatism.

'Can I take the glasses off at school?' I asked.

'No,' said Mr Samuels. 'All the time means all the time.'

Some girls suit glasses, but I don't. They look really weird on my face and make my eyes look tiny. Also, I need special corrective lenses, so I can't wear colourful, nice frames. Just horrible adult ones.

I wanted to burst into tears in the optician's chair. I know it sounds pathetic, but I felt like my world was ending.

Mum was upset too, but she put on a sort of false, bright voice and told me about all the famous people who wear glasses. Then Mr Samuels fitted the glasses and told me not to take them off until bedtime. I had to walk out of the opticians with the stupid, ugly things on my face.

Truthfully, I could see a lot better with the glasses on and my eyes didn't ache as much. But every time I saw myself in a shop window, I wanted to burst into tears.

When we got home, I begged not to wear the glasses at school.

'Can't I just put them on when I watch TV?' I pleaded. 'That's when I get the headaches. I'm fine at school.'

Mum said she'd think about it, but Dad said no way.

'If the optician said you have to wear them every day, you have to wear them every day,' he said.

'But what about dancing?' I asked. 'Miss Miel might not

pick me for the contest if I don't look professional. Professional dancers don't wear glasses.'

'There's no such thing as a professional dancer,' said Dad. 'And that contest is to win a scholarship for a dance school in London. Do you really want to leave St Valentine's and all your friends?'

'The scholarship is just one prize,' I said. 'But there are big cash prizes for every winning squad. I can put the money towards university fees.'

'You have to wear those glasses, Lottie,' said Dad. 'Even when you're dancing. And every day at school.'

I nodded along, but I have no intention of doing what Dad says.

Usually, I follow all the rules, but when it comes to glasses ... well, forget it. I'm not wearing those ugly things to school every day and *definitely* not during dance practice.

The moment I leave the house tomorrow, I'm taking my glasses off and hiding them in my school bag. I just hope Farrah doesn't see me doing it.

Farrah is my best friend, but I know she'll tease me about my glasses. She hones in on anything that looks different and makes jokes about it. It's like a superpower she has.

If Farrah wasn't so perfect looking, she wouldn't get away with half the things she says. She has a really angelic face, big blue eyes and freckles. Farrah doesn't *look* unkind, you know? But she is sometimes.

The main thing Farrah teases me about is being young for my age. She's always like, 'Lottie, when are you going to *grow up* and get your own phone? Why can't you wear a skirt above the knee like *everyone* else?'

Or she'll talk to Primrose and Sophie about adult movies

I'm not allowed to watch, and then say, 'Oh, sorreee Lottie. This is a grown-up conversation, no children allowed.'

And they all start giggling.

It's so unfair because it's not my fault Dad is so strict.

It doesn't help that Primrose and Sophie laugh at everything Farrah says. I think they're worried that if they don't join in, Farrah will say something mean about them next. But it doesn't work, because Farrah teases those girls too. Especially Sophie.

Farrah will say things like, 'Come on Sophie, we're all going to jump off a cliff. You're coming, right?'

And Sophie will say, 'Sure!' and not even realise it's a joke until everyone starts laughing.

Other than the teasing, Farrah and I get along really well.

No friendship is perfect.

SCARLETT

I made a really great dinner tonight – Japanese noodles in miso soup.

Mum didn't come home in time to eat it with me, so I put a bowl in the microwave for her to heat up.

While I was eating alone in the kitchen, the doorbell rang. I answered, chopsticks in hand, and found a large, blonde woman waving like a maniac.

'Hiiiiieee.' The woman held out a box of Dairy Milk chocolates. 'You must be Scarlett. I'm Kelly Turner. Your mother's friend.'

'Hello there.' I smiled. 'Are you married to the man who sold us the house? Doug Turner?'

Kelly nodded and put the chocolates in my free hand.

'These are for you. We meant to give them earlier, but since you've been too busy to come over ... well ... welcome.'

'Too busy to come over?' I said. 'I didn't know we'd been invited anywhere.'

Kelly gave a high-pitched laugh. 'Well, of course! Doug and I always invite over new families. And you're in our daughter's class, so we had an extra-special reason. Farrah has told us so much about you. She says you're in all the top sets. Maybe you'd like to *hang out* with Farrah some time?'

'Are you sure Farrah would like that?' I asked.

Kelly gave another screechy laugh. 'Of course! Why? Have the two of you had problems or something?'

'No,' I said. 'But Farrah is friends with Lottie, and ... well, Lottie hasn't exactly been friendly.'

'Oh *yes*,' Kelly whispered, eyes bright and manic. 'We've had problems with Lottie too. She can be a bit possessive. Her parents are lovely but ... Lottie has a strong personality.'

Jamie came downstairs then, a bottled beer in his hand.

'What's this?' he said. 'A party on the doorstep and everyone's invited?'

Kelly laughed again. 'Jamie! How are you settling in? I was just about to tell Scarlett that we only live a few houses away. So if she ever wants to hang out with Farrah, we're not far.'

'You must have psychic powers,' said Jamie. 'We were thinking about inviting you over. How about a barbecue this Saturday?'

'This Saturday?' Kelly gave a little squeal. 'That sounds wonderful. I'd love Farrah to meet new people.' She lowered her voice. 'She spends too much time with the same girls, and not all of them are good for her.'

'It's a date.' Jamie grabbed Kelly's hand and shook it. 'And how about Scarlett and Farrah have a sleepover after the barbecue? What do you think, Scarlett?' He gave me a wink. 'A friend staying over?'

'Great!' Kelly gave a little jump and clapped her hands. 'Farrah would love that. I'll tell her as soon as I get home.'

I wished Jamie hadn't suggested the sleepover. Sleepovers are for really good friends, not people you hardly know. It all felt a little weird and full-on. But I could hardly say no with Farrah's mother standing there. I didn't want to sound unfriendly.

LOTTIE

Oh my god.

The new girl is a total psychopath.

Farrah just called. Scarlett has invited her for a sleepover this weekend.

A sleepover!

That's something you do with really good friends.

Poor Farrah is dreading it.

'Why didn't you say no?' I asked.

'I wasn't there to say no,' said Farrah. 'Mum said yes for me. She is totally obsessed with the new family, because they bought that big house.'

Farrah's parents are sort of shallow like that. They like to get to know wealthy people because it helps Doug sell more houses. At least, that's what Mum says.

'But you're still coming to the park with us on Saturday afternoon, right?' I asked. 'We need to do as much dance practice as possible.'

'I'm so bored with dancing right now,' said Farrah. 'It's all we ever do. And the contest is over a *month* away. You know Miss Miel will put us forward. No one else from our school ever applies.'

'Because they're not in our league,' I said. 'But if they see our standards slip, they might try their luck. Only *one* squad from our school can go forward, Farrah. We need to make sure it's us.'

'Look,' said Farrah. 'I can't come to the park on Saturday because I'm going to a barbecue at Scarlett's house,'

'No way,' I said. 'You're hanging out with the new girl all afternoon too? Oh my god, Farrah. Can't you make an excuse and get out of it?'

'No,' said Farrah. 'Mum would kill me. She's really happy we've been invited over. She wants me and the new girl to be bestest friends.'

'I hope you can make up the practice time,' I said. 'Or we might have to find someone else.'

I hung up then, feeling really angry.

First, Scarlett tries to push her way into my dance squad. Now she's moving in on my best friend. It's like she's obsessed with me or something.

Why can't she just leave me alone?

SCARLETT

It was a long first week at St Valentine's.

By the time Saturday came, I just wanted to FaceTime my New York friends, practise dance routines from YouTube and eat ice cream. But instead, I had to do the whole barbecue sleepover thing with Farrah.

I honestly was grateful to Jamie for helping out, but ... I mean, it was all kind of weird. And I could tell Farrah thought so too.

The barbecue was okay.

Farrah's parents brought a whole load of food and beer,

and kept oohing and aahing at our house, saying how fabulous it was.

Kelly was funny. She was sort of dressed like a wedding guest, in this silk pink dress with a matching hat. Doug wore a gold watch with diamonds on it and a white suit with a lilac shirt. I liked them both – they were really friendly.

Farrah wore denim cut-offs and sunglasses. Her blonde hair was princess braided. She didn't seem as impressed by our house as her parents and kept saying, 'Why is it so *messy*?'

When I showed Farrah my bedroom and walk-in closet, she said, 'How come you dress so badly, when you have so many great clothes?'

I looked down at my loose jeans and hand-printed shirt. I've never made much effort with my clothes. I just wear what feels comfortable. With a mother like mine, there's not much room for anyone else to care about their appearance.

'One of my New York friends made me this t-shirt,' I said, looking down.

'So it's like *home*made?' Farrah scrunched up her pretty face.

'What's wrong with homemade?' I asked.

'Everyone will think you're ... poor or something,' said Farrah. 'Your mother looks great. Why don't you dress like her?'

'Because I don't want to waste my life worrying about my appearance,' I said.

'But you're so pretty,' said Farrah. 'And *look* at all the great clothes you have.' She went inside my closet and clicked hangers back and forth. 'It's super-duper designer cool. I mean, *really* cool.'

'One of my Mum's friends was a buyer for department stores,' I explained. 'She got lots of free clothes. She gave me all the teen stuff. Mum's always trying to get me to wear them, but ... well, like I said. I don't want to be like my Mum. If you knew her, you'd understand why.'

'You should definitely wear these clothes,' said Farrah, pulling out a black dress and holding it against me. 'And you should do something with your hair, too. It's really messy.'

'I'm okay with messy,' I said. 'It's how it grows.'

Farrah shrugged. 'Weird.'

When the barbecue was ready, Jamie put on his bright red chef hat and waved his light-sabre BBQ tongs around.

'Zhuum! Zhuuum!'

'Why is Jamie being so crazy?' sneered Farrah.

Kelly gave a high-pitched laugh, but she didn't tell Farrah off. Mum would have killed me for saying something like that.

When Farrah saw our swimming pool, I could tell she was disappointed.

'It doesn't have any water in it,' she said.

'I know,' I admitted. 'We need to get it cleaned first.'

'Well, let me know when it's ready,' said Farrah. 'We can be swimming buddies. I bet you could have the best pool parties. What do you think?'

I said I thought that was a great idea.

Things with Farrah got better after that. She started asking me all about New York and the dance contests I entered. Then Farrah and I made up a dance routine on the lawn.

'You're a really good dancer,' said Farrah. 'Shame you can't join our dance squad. But there's just no way. Lottie would never say yes.'

I could have danced all afternoon, but Farrah got bored after twenty minutes.

'Hey,' she said. 'Why don't we invite the girls over and watch movies?'

'Which girls?' I asked.

'Lottie and the girls,' said Farrah. 'Everyone.'

'Lottie doesn't like me,' I said.

'Lottie doesn't like anyone new,' said Farrah. 'She was the same with me.'

I shrugged. 'Okay. We can invite them over.'

Farrah called the girls, but none of them wanted to come.

'It's because of Lottie,' Farrah explained. 'Lottie doesn't like you, so the other girls don't like you either.'

'Why doesn't Lottie like me?' I asked. 'I barely even know her.'

Farrah shrugged. 'She didn't like me when I moved here either. But I think you're really cool. Hey, why don't I call for you on Monday morning? We can walk to school together.'

'Sure,' I said. 'That sounds great.'

'Actually, wait.' Farrah thought for a moment. 'I'd better check with Lottie first.'

'Can't you decide for yourself?' I asked.

'Are you kidding me?' said Farrah. 'With Lottie around, it's not worth the headache.'

I asked if Lottie was Farrah's friend or her boss.

Farrah laughed. 'A little bit of both.'

In the end, the sleepover was fun. Farrah and I drank Coca Cola and got the giggles. And we did more dancing and watched music videos. Farrah is more like me than Amina and Marianne. But it feels like, with Lottie around, there's not much chance Farrah and I will ever become good friends.

LOTTIE

On Monday morning, Farrah filled me in on the barbecue sleepover with Scarlett.

'Scarlett's house was really messy,' said Farrah. 'And the swimming pool was mouldy. Oh, and her stepdad is totally weird. Scarlett asked if we could call for her on the way to school. Can we?'

'Are you kidding me?' I said. 'Scarlett's not part of our group.'

'I wasn't part of your group, once upon a time,' said Farrah. 'Scarlett's a really good dancer. Maybe we should give her a chance.'

'What are you talking about?' I laughed. 'There was no group until you came along. Look, we can't call for Scarlett. She'll make us late. She was late twice last week. Didn't you notice her waltzing in halfway through the register? Talk about full of herself. I can't hang out with latecomers, Farrah. I'm head girl.'

We called for Primrose and Sophie on the way to school. Then, on the way up the country path, I heard someone calling. I turned to see Scarlett a little way behind. It looked like she was trying to catch us up.

'Hey,' I told my friends. 'Let's walk faster. We don't want to be late.'

SCARLETT

I really hoped Farrah would call for me on Monday morning. Sure, she was a little rude at the barbeque, but I could tell that was just her personality. And we really did have fun in the end. But she didn't turn up. I guess Lottie must have told her no. So I ended up walking in alone.

As I was heading up the country track, I saw Farrah, Lottie and two other girls walking up ahead.

'Hey!' I called. 'Wait up!'

Lottie turned and saw me.

I waved, but Lottie didn't wave back. Then she grabbed Farrah's arm and walked faster.

By the time I got to school, I felt so upset.

What had I ever done to Lottie Collins? Why did she hate me so much?

I thought Farrah might be friendlier at school, but she was weird. She smiled and said hello, but that was all. It was like the barbecue sleepover had never happened.

When I got home, I sent messages to all my old friends in New York. Then I phoned Dad, but he didn't answer. Mum still wasn't home, so I ended up crying to Jamie about the girls at school.

'Farrah said she might walk with me this morning,' I told Jamie. 'She lives, like, three seconds away. But she left without me. And she ignored me all day. There's this girl, Lottie. People call her a queen bee. Farrah is too scared to be friendly with Lottie around.'

'Oh, who cares about Farrah,' said Jamie. 'Her parents were dull. They may as well have written 'we love money' across their chests. And no woman over the age of twenty should wear sequin shoes. Find better people to hang around with.'

'You're missing the point,' I said. 'Lottie doesn't like me, and the other girls worship her. They won't be my friend while she's around.'

Jamie thought for a moment. 'Okay. So throw an

amazing party and invite every girl in your year. I'm thinking fruit cocktails, live band, karaoke. Temporary tattoos, laser lights, disco smoke. Make it as fantastic as you are. And the whole school will fall in love with you, including this Lottie girl. You'll see. Hey, we can design the invitations right now.'

One thing I'll say about Jamie – he thinks big.

'But it's not my birthday until next month,' I said.

'So?' said Jamie. 'This can be a settling in party. And when you've decided who all the cool kids are, invite them to your birthday.'

Jamie and I had a fun time designing the invitations on his Mac, and afterwards, I felt a lot better. Okay, so the sleepover with Farrah hadn't gone so well. But a party was different. Much less awkward.

Once I'd printed the invitations, I headed over to Farrah's house, invitation in hand.

I knew Farrah's address, because Kelly told us about their house 'with pillars, just a few doors down from you' so many times during the barbecue.

Farrah's house looked nice. Neat and modern, with those perfect, little round lollypop trees by the front door. The pillars were a little out of place on such a small house, but I guess Kelly and Doug like to look grand.

When I knocked on the door, Farrah answered.

'Oh hey,' she said. 'Did I leave something at your house?'

'I have an invitation for you,' I replied. 'I'm throwing a really fun party in my garden next Saturday. We'll have fruit cocktails and stuff.'

'Who else is invited?' Farrah asked.

'Everyone,' I said. 'I'm inviting the whole homeroom. I mean, *form* room. I'll give out the rest of the invites tomorrow.'

'You're inviting Lottie?' asked Farrah.

'Yes,' I said. 'Even Lottie.'

Farrah shrugged and took her invitation. 'Okay. Sounds fun.'

I left Farrah's house with mixed feelings. Farrah had been pretty rude about the invite, but she'd said yes to the party. So all in all, it was good news. And hopefully, Lottie would appreciate the party invitation too. It was about time she gave me a chance.

LOTTIE

Farrah just called.

She told me that Scarlett is throwing a huge party next weekend and inviting every girl in our form.

'Scarlett's giving the invitations out tomorrow,' Farrah told me. 'She gave me mine early because ... well, I suppose she thinks I'm a special friend.'

Farrah gave a little snort then, like, *what a pathetic idiot*.

It's so obvious what Scarlett's doing. She's giving Farrah's invitation ahead of time to try and win her friendship. But Farrah is *my* best friend. Why can't Scarlett just find her own friends and leave us alone?

'Did you say Scarlett's party was this Saturday?' I asked.

'Yes,' said Farrah.

'That's bad timing,' I said. 'Because I'm having an exclusive party that exact same day. *And* a secret sleepover. I meant to send out invitations ages ago, but I've been so busy with the opticians and everything, I totally forgot.'

'How did it go at the opticians?' Farrah asked. 'Aren't you supposed to wear glasses or something?'

'Not really,' I said. 'I mean, he sort of gave me glasses. But I don't have to wear them much. Hardly ever, really.'

That was a total lie. I was wearing my ugly, man glasses while I talked to Farrah on the phone.

'Can't you change the date of your party?' said Farrah. 'I've already said yes to Scarlett.'

'Sorry,' I lied. 'I've had the invitations printed. But it's up to you. You could go to Scarlett's party with all the desperate girls. Or you could come and have fun with your real friends. *And* you get to stay for the secret sleepover. Because you're part of the A-Squad.'

Farrah took about two seconds to make her decision. She was coming to my sleepover party instead.

Once Farrah said yes, I called Primrose and Sophie.

'I'm having a party next Saturday,' I told them. 'It's going to be a really fun makeover party with a secret sleepover. We'll do nail polish and a foot spa. Then the B-girls will go home, and the A-girls will stay for Domino's pizza and a sleepover.'

Primrose got really excited: 'I LOVE Domino's pizza! Can we have pepperoni?'

Sophie said it sounded like fun and asked what she should wear.

'Ballet tutus,' I said. 'I'm doing a pink ballerina theme.'

Once I hung up the phone, I found Mum in the kitchen, loading the dishwasher.

'I'm having issues,' I told Mum. 'The new girl is trying to steal Farrah away. Honestly, she acts like she owns the whole school.'

Mum laughed. 'You have nothing to worry about. Everyone at that school loves you. You're head girl.'

'But Scarlett already invited Farrah for a sleepover at her big house,' I said. 'How can I compete with a mansion and a swimming pool?'

'A sleepover?' said Mum. 'Already? That's fast work. The new family have only been here five minutes.'

'Exactly,' I said. 'Scarlett's totally trying to steal my friends.'

'I bet the sleepover was Kelly's idea,' said Mum. 'No doubt she and Doug are cosying up to the new family, hoping to sell a few more houses.'

'Can I have my own sleepover this weekend?' I asked.

'Well, that's a good idea,' said Mum. 'Do something positive.'

'And a party too?' I asked. 'Just a little one. A few extra friends in the afternoon. And my best friends sleeping over?'

'Oh, why not?' said Mum. 'You work so hard. You deserve a little celebration.'

'Thanks, Mum.' I gave her a big hug. That's when I caught a glimpse of myself in the bi-folding doors.

Uh oh.

My glasses. I have to wear them at home because Mum and Dad are there. But my friends still don't know about them, because I take them off when I leave the house.

I took a deep breath. 'Mum, do I have to wear my glasses at the party?'

'Well, of course you do,' said Mum. 'You have to wear them all the time.'

'*Please* Mum,' I said. 'It'll only be for a day. And party clothes just don't look the same with glasses.'

Mum gave me a long look. 'You are wearing your glasses at school, aren't you?'

I gave a quick nod.

Mum sighed. 'Well. I suppose it's okay. Your father will never agree to it, but he's going to the cricket this Saturday. So it'll be our secret, okay?'

Cassandra poked her head into the kitchen then. She

was dressed in tennis gear, shining blonde hair in a perfect ponytail.

'Are you keeping secrets from Dad again?' she asked.

Mum went red. 'No. You must have misheard us.'

'Because Lottie's glasses are for her health,' said Cassandra. 'She's supposed to wear them all the time.'

'Don't tell your father,' Mum warned. 'Or there'll be another big argument. Sometimes the easiest way is just to keep quiet.'

Cassandra looked like she wanted to say something, but then she snapped her mouth shut and walked away.

By bedtime, I'd called half the girls in our form and told them about the party. They were all thrilled to be invited. I even invited Marianne – who I must say was very rude. She asked why I was calling, told me I'd always been mean to her (Mean! I hardly even notice her) and said she wouldn't be able to come.

Well, it's her loss.

I didn't invite the *whole* class. Obviously. I'm not a desperate show-off, like Scarlett.

Mum says you should keep parties on the small side, to make yourself seem more in demand.

I couldn't agree more.

SCARLETT

Absolutely horrible day.

I turned up at school with my party invitations and a huge smile on my face. The moment Mrs Singh finished the register, I jumped up from my desk and started handing out invites.

Some of the girls looked really awkward, which was

weird. Then I gave Amina her invite, and I found out the reason for the weirdness.

'I'm so sorry, Scarlett.' Amina looked up at me with big, earnest brown eyes. 'I can't come. I've already said yes to Lottie's party. It's on the same day.'

I stared at her, open-mouthed.

'*Lottie's* party?' I said. 'Lottie's having a party on the same day as mine?'

Amina nodded. 'She called last night to tell me.'

'She called me too,' said Marianne. 'It was very strange. Lottie never invites me to anything.'

I looked down at my handful of invitations, which were now shaking.

'Lottie's done this on purpose,' I said. 'Farrah must have told her about my party. So now Lottie's planned one on the exact same day.'

Amina gave me a kind smile. 'Lottie wouldn't do that. She is competitive, but ... I think this was just a coincidence.'

'Well, let's find out.' I marched up to Lottie, who was sitting with Farrah at the front of the class. Primrose and Sophie sat around Lottie's desk, like servants gathering around their queen.

'Hey, Lottie.' I said. 'You're having a party this Saturday, right?'

Lottie looked scared for a moment. Then she pulled herself together. 'Sorry I didn't invite you, but I don't even know you.'

'Farrah,' I said. 'Did you tell Lottie about my party?'

Farrah looked scared too. 'Why's everyone looking at me?'

'Just answer the question,' I said. 'Did you tell Lottie about my party?'

'Yes, she did,' said Lottie. 'I'm her best friend. And it was hardly a secret. You're inviting the whole class.' Then she muttered under her breath, '*Talk about desperate*.'

Primrose gave an awkward giggle.

'Are you coming to my party, Farrah?' I asked. 'Like you said you would?'

'Um ...' Farrah laughed and looked at Lottie.

'She can't make it,' said Lottie. 'She's coming to my party instead. Which, by the way, I planned ages ago. There was just a problem with the invitations. Sorreee it's on the same day as yours, but that's life sometimes.'

I gave Lottie a look. A really angry 'I want to kill you' look. At first, Lottie tried to eyeball me back, but then she looked away.

'You did this on purpose,' I said.

'Oh my god, Scarlett,' said Lottie. 'Talk about paranoid. SUMO. Shut up and move on.'

Lottie's friends giggled. I could handle Lottie alone, but all those other girls laughing along ... I felt so small and stupid.

I did something embarrassing then. I grabbed all my party invitations from the desks, ran into the cloakroom and burst into tears.

Maybe it was kind of desperate to invite the whole class. I don't know. I was just trying to make friends.

I didn't want anyone to see me crying, but after a few minutes, Amina came into the cloakroom with Mrs Singh.

'Amina says you're upset over a party,' said Mrs Singh. 'Do you want to tell me about it?'

I sniffed and wiped my eyes. 'It's fine,' I said. 'Totally fine.'

Amina tried to explain. 'Lottie is having a party the same day as Scarlett. I'm sure it's just an innocent mistake, but Lottie isn't being kind about it. She told Scarlett to shut up and move on.'

I gave Amina a grateful smile.

'Oh, that's not very nice,' said Mrs Singh. 'Is it an early birthday party, or something, Scarlett? You're a summer birthday, aren't you?'

I shook my head. 'My birthday is a month away. This is just a party.'

'Why don't we call Lottie in and see if one of you can change your party date?' Mrs Singh suggested.

'There's no way I'm having a party now,' I said. 'No one will come.'

'Okay.' Mrs Singh put a large arm around my shoulder. 'I can see you're upset. It's hard being the new girl. Did Lottie invite you to her party?'

I shook my head, feeling totally pathetic.

'Well, maybe that's something we can suggest to Lottie,' said Mrs Singh. 'She's a nice girl. I promise. Even if she seems a little spiky.'

I didn't want to go to Lottie's stupid party, but I couldn't tell Mrs Singh that. Otherwise, she'd think I was being difficult.

Mrs Singh checked her watch. 'Let's get this settled before the end of registration. I'll go get Lottie.'

I wiped away tears, but I knew my eyes were red. It was so embarrassing.

Lottie looked nervous when she came into the cloakroom. She started talking at one hundred miles an hour.

'I haven't done anything wrong, Mrs Singh. It wasn't my fault. There was just a problem with the invitations. I thought I'd ordered them ages ago, but I must have made a mistake because they didn't turn up, and then when Farrah told me about Scarlett's party, that's when I remembered.'

It was such an obvious lie.

'You're not in trouble, Lottie,' Mrs Singh smiled. 'But we're trying to help Scarlett get settled in. You're a friendly girl. Might you have space at your party for Scarlett too?'

Lottie's pointy face went all tight, and she mumbled something about not knowing me all that well.

'But isn't that what parties are about?' said Mrs Singh. 'So you can *get* to know each other?'

'I'm sorry, Mrs Singh,' said Lottie. 'But my mum has already ordered the personalised party bags.'

Mrs Singh laughed. 'My goodness. When I was your age, we were lucky to have a birthday party once a year with a balloon and a piece of cake. There were none of these parties for no reason, with party bags. Listen, Lottie. You're our lower-school head girl. You want to set a good example, don't you?'

Lottie gave a reluctant nod.

'Lovely.' Mrs Singh stood up and checked her watch again. 'Now, do you two want to shake hands and move forwards?'

Lottie and I both knew the answer to that.

No.

But we shook hands, even though it felt totally wrong.

'Lottie, will you give Scarlett a proper invitation by the end of the week?' Mrs Singh urged. 'So she doesn't feel left out?'

Lottie had to say yes to that. Of course, we both knew that Lottie didn't have any proper invitations yet. Because she only decided to have a party when she found out about mine.

LOTTIE

Oh my god, Scarlett is SUCH a drama queen. Hiding in the cloakroom like that and *crying*.

I have never, EVER cried at school and I never will. If you cry, you show everyone you're weak.

I'm furious with Scarlett for getting me in trouble. I *never* get in trouble. And THEN Mrs Singh made me invite Scarlett to my party.

Totally unbelievable!

All the girls agree that my party is my own business. I shouldn't have to invite anyone I don't want to.

Do you know what was really funny? Mrs Singh said Scarlett and I could be great friends because we're both 'strong characters'.

Ha!

Scarlett was hiding in the cloakroom in tears. How is that a strong character? And as for the two of us being friends ... who is Mrs Singh kidding? I'm head girl. Scarlett can't even get the school uniform right. We are nothing alike.

I have to admit, I'm glad Mrs Singh believed I'd made an innocent mistake with my party date. Being head girl has its advantages. People tend to think the best of you.

At dinner that evening, I told my family about all the drama at school.

'It was so unfair,' I said. 'Scarlett started crying and Mrs Singh felt sorry for her.'

'Honestly,' said Mum. 'What are they teaching this girl? That all she has to do is burst into tears and she'll get whatever she wants?'

'Inviting one extra girl to your party is no big deal,' said Cassandra, piling steamed broccoli onto her plate. 'You're lucky, Lottie. You grew up in Hiverstock. You've never had to be the new girl. I had to push my way into school friendship groups, like Scarlett. I really appreciated it when people were friendly.'

'Think of it as Christian charity,' said Dad.

'It's nothing to do with charity, Robert,' said Mum. 'If this girl gets a party invite because she cried, she'll think she's won.'

Dad got really angry then.

'Life isn't all about winning and losing, Nicola.'

Mum and Dad had a huge argument after that.

Dad was bellowing: 'How many times do I have to say it, Nicola? It's about doing the right thing? Not *appearing* to do the right thing.'

Cassandra and I went up to her bedroom and closed the door.

'What's your problem with the new girl?' Cassandra asked. 'Why don't you want her at your party?'

'She's a total huge drama queen,' I said. 'And a show-off.'

'Maybe she's just trying to be seen,' said Cassandra.

'No, she's trying to steal my friends,' I said. 'That's why I had this party in the first place. Because Scarlett invited *my* friends to her great big house this weekend. So I had to do something.'

'If you have to fight for your friends, they're not really your friends,' said Cassandra.

An hour later, Mum came upstairs.

'I'm sorry about the arguing, girls,' she said. 'You know what your father's like.'

'You need two people to have an argument,' said Cassandra.

Mum ignored her. 'Listen, Lottie. I've just spoken to Kelly. She says there was some confusion over party dates. Apparently, Scarlett is throwing a party next Saturday too.'

I shrugged.

Cassandra gave me a look then, but I ignored her.

'I imagine that's why Scarlett felt upset,' Mum continued. 'All the girls will obviously come to your party instead of hers.'

'Well, obviously,' I said.

'I don't want anyone thinking you're unkind or thoughtless, Lottie,' said Mum. 'You should hand deliver Scarlett's party invitation right now. To show you're a good person. Hurry up. You don't want to look like the bad guy.'

SCARLETT

Lottie just showed up on my doorstep with a party invitation. Only it wasn't really a party invitation. It was a torn piece of paper covered in pencil scrawl.

'I'm sorry you got so upset about my party,' said Lottie, shoving the paper into my hand. 'Everyone says I should invite you because you're new and you got upset. So I'm inviting you.'

I looked down at the crumpled note.

Lottie hadn't even written my name at the top. Instead, she'd put: 'New Girl'. Like my name offended her in some way.

I was furious and nearly told Lottie to get lost. But I knew that's exactly what she wanted me to do.

'Will you be able to come to the party?' Lottie asked. 'Or will you be busy?'

'I can come,' I said. 'Because I've cancelled my party now. Thank you for being *so* friendly.'

After Lottie left, Mum appeared, glass of wine in hand. She was wearing a bright yellow silk kaftan, with a geometric headscarf artfully tied around her shiny, black hair. Her lipstick and nails were bold, red and perfect.

Farrah's right – Mum does always look great.

'See?' Mum said. 'I told you it would be easy to make friends. One week, and you've already been invited to a party.'

'You don't get it,' I said.

Mum gave me a look. 'Darling, there's no need to be rude.'

'Why are you out here, anyway?' I asked. 'You're never usually interested in my friends.'

'Kelly Turner is coming over for a glass of wine,' said Mum. 'I thought that was her at the door.'

'Kelly?' I said. 'As in Farrah's mother?'

'That's right,' said Mum. 'So you can't accuse me of not being interested in you, darling. I'm getting to know the parent of one of your friends.'

'Farrah isn't one of my friends,' I said. 'If you were interested in me, you'd know that.'

Mum glared at me, and I knew I'd gone too far. Luckily, at that moment the doorbell rang. It was Kelly, holding a bottle of Moët champagne.

Mum calls Moët champagne 'the cheap kind', but she graciously took the bottle and welcomed Kelly into the house.

Kelly gave me a big, warm smile when she saw me hanging around the hallway.

I smiled back. I was really glad to see her because she'd just saved me from being shouted at.

'How are you, angel?' Kelly asked. 'Settling in well at school?'

'Yes, Mrs Turner,' I said.

'Oh, call me Kelly,' said Kelly. 'Mrs Turner sounds so old. Farrah tells me you were having a party this Saturday, but Lottie is having a party on the same day.'

I nodded and looked at my feet, feeling the crumpled party invitation between my fingers.

Kelly put a gentle hand on my shoulder.

'Lottie can be a sneaky one,' she said. 'She's been very mean to Farrah in the past. Keep your chin up and don't take any nonsense. That girl can be a real bully.'

LOTTIE

I am SO stressed.

Throwing a party at such short notice is more difficult than I thought. There are only three days until Saturday, and I need at least three more weeks. Maybe four.

I've ordered all the party supplies, but some things won't arrive until Saturday morning.

Major headache.

The pink cowboy hats *should* arrive tomorrow. They come in packs of eight, so there won't be enough for Scarlett. I'm not ordering a whole extra set of hats just for her.

I can't bake the cakes until party day, because otherwise, they won't be fresh.

The invitations – well, right now they don't exist. I may not bother with them at all, since I've invited everyone in person anyway.

The only thing I have ready are the placeholders. I made them last night and wrote the girls' names on them. Then I drew cute little hearts and flowers on everyone's card

– except Scarlett's. It would have been weird to draw hearts or cute pictures on her card because we're not friends. So I just wrote Scarlett's name and left it at that.

Scarlett doesn't deserve cute pictures anyway. She was so ungrateful for her party invitation. Who does she think she is?

On the way to school, I told the girls how rude Scarlett had been when I delivered her invite.

'Scarlett barely even said thank you,' I told them. 'I mean, she did. But in a rude way. Like, *thanks* for being *so* friendly.'

'You would have thought she'd be happy,' said Primrose. 'She made a big deal of not being invited, didn't she?'

I nodded. 'A really big deal. She was crying and everything.'

'How is the party planning going?' Sophie asked.

'I'm *so* behind schedule,' I told her. 'Half the party supplies won't arrive until Saturday. And the pink hearts aren't due until Saturday afternoon. They're the centrepiece of the whole thing. If they don't turn up, I don't know what I'll do.'

'Why didn't you order them earlier?' Sophie asked. 'You're usually so organised.'

'I've just had a lot going on,' I said quickly. 'With the opticians and everything. So I sort of forgot.'

'Have you seen the optician again now?' asked Sophie.

'Mmm-hmm,' I said.

'And what did he say?' said Sophie.

'Oh, nothing much,' I said airily.

We walked on in silence after that, and I thought about my glasses, jogging along in my school bag.

I wish I could be honest with my friends, but I just can't

risk it. If my parents find out I'm not wearing my glasses at school, they'll kill me.

Sophie might keep my secret, but most likely she'd tell Primrose. And Primrose would tell Farrah, who would tell the world.

Cassandra says that good friends are trustworthy and keep secrets, but that hasn't been my experience. If I tell my friends anything embarrassing, the whole school knows the next day.

SCARLETT

By the time Saturday came around, I'd convinced myself that Lottie's party might be fun after all. At the very least, Lottie would see that I'm a nice person and not a big cry baby.

I'm not great at dressing up for parties, but I remembered what Farrah said about my clothes. Maybe I should wear more of the fancy stuff.

At my New York school, the idea was to look like you hadn't tried all that hard. But around here, the girls look like fashion models. Everything matches.

I ended up wearing this big, blue ballgown thing with red shoes. It didn't look quite right, so I added a black pearl necklace, plastic bangles and an ankle bracelet. That didn't look right either, but by then it was time to go.

As I walked to Lottie's house, I thought, *maybe this dress is a bit much with the shoes and everything.*

My hair was a little crazy, too. Brushing it had somehow made it bigger. I wish I was one of those girls who can do braids and all that kind of stuff, but I'm not.

Lottie's house turned out to be really near mine. I mean,

honestly. I could throw a stone from my bedroom window and hit the fake grass on her front lawn.

Mum would say Lottie's home is 'nouveau riche', which is another way of saying 'low class.' But I liked the look of Lottie's house: the perfectly square bushes in the front garden, freshly painted walls and sparkling clean windows. It was obviously well looked after, you know? Not like our house, with knee-high grass, a mouldy swimming pool and cracks all over the place.

I put on my best, friendliest smile as I knocked on Lottie's front door.

Lottie's mother answered, and gave me a nervous smile in return.

'You must be Scarlett.' Mrs Collins had the same pointed nose and piercing blue eyes as Lottie. 'You've moved into the big house on the corner, haven't you? I hope you're settling in okay.'

Mrs Collins was what Mum would call 'an English rose'. Light brown-blonde hair, creamy skin and a flowery dress. Sort of boring, but she's not going to offend anyone. Her face was very tense and her eyes looked frightened.

'Yes, we're settling in fine, Mrs Collins,' I said. 'Thank you for asking.'

'My word,' said Mrs Collins. 'What an interesting outfit. Did you get those clothes in New York?'

I looked down at my dress, pearls, bangles and shoes.

'Um ... yes. One of Mum's friends is a buyer for Barney's and ... um ... well, she gets this stuff for me. I don't really know how to wear it, though.' I gave a little laugh.

Mrs Collins nodded. 'How are you settling into the school, Scarlett? Everything okay? Making friends?'

'I'm trying,' I said.

'I'm sure you'll find your group,' said Mrs Collins. 'Well. Come on through.'

Mrs Collins ushered me into the kitchen. Pink food, confetti and giant paper hearts were laid on a dining table, and girls milled around, eating cakes. Amina was among them, dressed in a baggy pink ballet tutu. Her hair was in its usual long braid under a pink cowboy hat. It felt good to see at least one friendly face.

Mum would have said the party room looked *like a ten-dollar Vegas wedding,* but I thought it was cool. And well organised. Lottie had obviously worked hard.

Then I noticed something. *All* the girls were wearing ballet tutus and pink cowboy hats.

Was there a dress code or something? And where had all the cowboy hats come from?

'Lottie,' Mrs Collins called. 'Come and welcome your guest.'

Lottie drifted towards me, a vision in pastel pink, and Mrs Collins scurried away to straighten the cake stand.

'Hello Scarlett,' said Lottie, looking me up and down. 'I don't have a cowboy hat for you, because you were a late invite. I didn't want to order a whole extra set. There would have been too many. And ... well, it looks like you're wearing everything in your wardrobe anyway. The last thing you need is another accessory.'

Someone sniggered.

'It's fine,' I said, trying to smile.

Amina appeared at my elbow, then.

'Scarlett, take my hat,' she said. 'It's hurting my head anyway.' She squashed her hat over my red curls before I could object.

Then Farrah came over. 'Oh my god, Scarlett,' she said,

between mouthfuls of cake. 'Are you wearing fancy dress or something? Don't you know there's a dress code?'

'No,' I said. 'I had no idea there's a dress code.'

'Lottie didn't tell you about the dress code?' said Amina. 'We're supposed to wear ballet tutus.'

I stared at Lottie. 'Why didn't you tell me?'

'There wasn't time to tell you,' Lottie snapped. 'Because you were a late invite.'

More girls gathered around in their pink ballet tutus, whispering about my outfit.

Why isn't she following the dress code? That's so rude. And what is she wearing?

I hate it when people whisper. It's so sneaky because if you call them up on it, they just say you heard it wrong.

Amina put a kind hand on my shoulder. 'Lottie should have told you about the dress code.'

'Okay, policewoman Jones,' said Farrah. 'Put your badge away. It's a party.'

Primrose snorted with laughter.

Amina rolled her eyes. 'Scarlett. Would you like some cake?'

'Um ... okay,' I said. But I didn't feel like eating.

While Amina and I were getting cake, Lottie clapped her hands together.

'People!' she announced. 'It's movie time. We're watching Pretty in Pink in the TV room.'

All the girls hurried into the next room, where there was a TV, a sofa and pink bunting.

At first, I didn't get why everyone was rushing. But when I got to the TV room, I understood. There was only one sofa in Lottie's lounge, and all the girls were trying to squash onto it. Farrah had already taken pride of place next to Lottie, and all the other girls were pushing themselves onto every available arm and cushion.

By the time I came into the room, there was no space left. I had to sit on the floor, squashed in among everyone's feet.

Amina jumped off the sofa arm and said: 'This is stupid. All of us squashed in. I'll sit with you, Scarlett. It's much more comfortable down there.'

It wasn't more comfortable, and we both knew it. But I appreciated what Amina was doing.

After the movie, we sat down for party food.

There were place settings. Yes. Place settings. Like a wedding. Every girl had colourful hearts, flowers and medals on her name card, except me. My card was cold and white, with just my name. Misspelt, of course, with just one 't'.

Naturally, Lottie sat me at the end of the table, away from all her best friends.

I fiddled with my plain white name card, watching all the other girls laugh and have fun in their matching pink tutus.

Why did Lottie hate me so much? I'd never done anything to her, and yet she was determined to be unkind.

Tears slid down my cheeks. At first, nobody noticed. Then Lottie's Mum came to 'refresh the pink lemonade'.

'Oh, Scarlett!' she said. 'Are you okay?'

I nodded, looking down. Everyone stared then. It was so embarrassing.

'But you're *crying*,' said Mrs Collins. Her eyes looked worried. They kept darting around the table, zooming in on anything that looked untidy – which I guess included my teary face.

'Are you feeling unwell?' Mrs Collins continued.

'Would you like me to call your parents and have them take you home?'

I shook my head. 'My mum has gone out for the day with Kelly Turner,' I said. 'And my stepdad has gone to London.'

Mrs Collins's eyes widened. 'Kelly has gone out with *your* mother?'

I nodded.

'Kelly never told me about that.' Mrs Collins frowned. 'I wonder ... well, I hope they're having a nice time. Where have they gone?'

'I think ... some sort of spa,' I sniffed.

'Right.' Mrs Collins looked thoughtful. 'I see.' Then she looked down the table. 'Girls! Scarlett is feeling upset. So let's make sure she feels extra-specially looked after. She *is* new here.'

When Mrs Collins left, Lottie said, 'What's your problem, Scarlett? You cried because I didn't invite you to my party. And now you're crying because you're here.'

'I just miss my friends in New York,' I said, pulling on a fake smile. 'I'm fine now.'

Not long after that, parents arrived to pick up their daughters.

Farrah, Primrose and Sophie didn't get picked up, though. They went into the lounge and whispered about a secret sleepover and Domino's pizza.

I had to walk home by myself because Mum doesn't do party pick-ups. She either tells me to walk home by myself or asks someone else to drop me off.

I didn't mind it. I was happy to leave that party as soon as possible.

What is wrong with Lottie Collins? Her life is totally

perfect. She lives with both her parents in a really nice house. She's pretty. She has loads of friends.

Why does she hate me so much?

LOTTIE

My party was okay. Not great, but okay.

It was annoying, having Scarlett there in her weird clothes. But all the party supplies arrived on time and the table looked beautiful.

The secret sleepover was not so fun.

Farrah can be such a princess sometimes. It was *my* sleepover. I should choose who goes where. But Farrah wouldn't stick to the rules. She totally refused to sleep in the double bed with me, saying she needed her own bed on the floor.

THEN Farrah wouldn't wear the pink pyjamas I bought her. She wanted to wear her own leopard-print pyjamas instead. It was so ungrateful because I'd bought her those pyjamas so we'd be matching.

Eventually, Mum came upstairs with a worried look in her eyes and asked if we were all getting along.

Cassandra called from her bedroom, 'Lottie's bossing everyone around. As per usual.'

All my friends giggled, which was so embarrassing.

I screamed at Cassandra, 'You're just jealous because you lost all *your* friends.'

Then Cassandra got really angry and stormed into my bedroom.

'Why aren't you wearing your glasses, Lottie?' she snapped. 'You're supposed to wear them *all* the time.'

'What?' Farrah had a weird smile on her face. 'You're supposed to wear glasses *all* the time, Lottie?'

'No,' I mumbled. 'Not all the time.'

'All the time,' said Cassandra. She flounced off and returned with my glasses case. 'Here you go, Lottie. You need your glasses if you're watching the iPad.' She threw the glasses case at me.

I could have killed her.

'Let's see your glasses, then,' said Farrah.

'I don't need to wear them all the time,' I said. 'Just ... TV and stuff.'

'Well, we're watching TV, aren't we?' said Farrah, pointing to the iPad.

All the girls watched me expectantly.

'Okay, fine.' I took the glasses out of the case and put them on.

'Oh my god,' Farrah roared. 'You look like such a nerd.'

Primrose got the giggles and couldn't stop. Sophie didn't say anything.

I whipped my glasses off and put them away. 'I don't need them, really,' I said. 'Cassandra was just being an idiot.'

Before we went to bed, Mum took lots of photos of us posing in our pyjamas. Then she sent the photos to all the mums on the WhatsApp secret sleepover group, along with shots of the party table and us wearing cowboy hats.

It looked like we were having the best time, even though truthfully, I wasn't.

Sometimes, when I see photos of my perfect parties, with all the lovely decorations, I wonder – did I actually have fun? Or does it just look that way to other people?

PART 2

RIVAL QUEENS

Over time, a queen bee lays fewer eggs. The other bees sense this and begin the process of replacing her.

SCARLETT

THE SUNDAY after Lottie's party, Jamie walked out on us. I'm not sure exactly *when* he left. All I know is that I woke up on Sunday morning and Mum was crying in her bedroom.

'Jamie's gone,' Mum sobbed. 'He didn't even say goodbye. What kind of man walks out on his children?'

But Mum is kidding herself if she thinks Jamie is any sort of father figure. I like Jamie, but he's like a teenager. Zara is more of a parent to me than he is, and she doesn't even live with us right now.

Mum spent all of Sunday in her bedroom. I tried to bring her food, but she wouldn't eat it. She only wanted 'very cold' white wine, and by the afternoon she'd drunk a whole bottle.

It's scary seeing your mum fall to pieces right in front of you. Especially when no one else is home.

I phoned Dad about fifty times, but the phone wasn't connecting for some reason – probably some international call thing. I emailed Dad too, but I know he doesn't check his emails over the weekend.

By late afternoon, I was so worried that I called Zara. I call my big sister most evenings, but hardly ever in the daytime because I know she studies. So we both knew it was an emergency.

Zara said she'd be on the first train to Hiverstock, and told me to hide the headache tablets. Mum took a whole packet of headache tablets years ago and ended up in hospital. I don't remember it, but Zara does.

An hour later, Zara turned up on the doorstep with a silver suitcase on wheels and designer sunglasses on her head. She looked really good. Her gleaming black hair was wrapped in a fashionable top-knot and her olive skin was suntanned and glowing.

Zara asked if I was okay.

'No,' I said.

'Sorry,' said Zara. Then she charged upstairs and into Mum's bedroom, slamming the door behind her. I followed and waited outside.

At first, I heard muffled voices. Then I put my ear to the door and heard Zara shout: 'When are you going to grow up and be a parent? Why did you have kids if you don't want to bring them up?'

'How can you be so heartless?' Mum wailed. 'Jamie has *left* me.'

'Don't tell me about having a heart,' said Zara. 'I don't think you have a heart at all.'

'I *do* have a heart, darling,' said Mum, in a dangerous voice. 'And if you're so concerned about your little sister, why don't you take her back to London with you?'

'I can't look after her either,' said Zara. 'I study and I work. Scarlett. SCARLETT! Are you out there?'

I opened the bedroom door. 'What?'

'Tell me about the girls at your school,' said Zara. 'Could you stay with any of them for a few days? While our mother gets herself together?'

'No way,' I said. 'I don't know anyone well enough to –'

'You know Kelly's daughter, Farrah,' said Mum. 'The two of you had a sleepover. And Kelly and I are getting along very well.'

'No way,' I said. 'No way am I staying with Farrah. She's best friends with Lottie and Lottie is awful.'

'It would just be for a few days, Scarlett,' said Mum. 'Zara's right. I'm in no state to take care of you right now.'

'Since when did you ever take care of her?' snapped Zara.

Mum ignored Zara and phoned Farrah's mother. I waited anxiously, not really sure what to wish for. I didn't want to stay with Farrah, but I didn't want to stay at home either. What I really wanted was to stay with Zara. I always feel warm and safe when my big sister is around. Sort of the opposite of how I feel with Mum.

Eventually, Mum hung up the phone.

'Scarlett?' she said. 'Pack some school clothes and an overnight bag. Kelly says she'll pick you up in ten minutes. You'll stay with the Turners until I'm feeling better.'

'How long will that be?' I asked.

'I'm not sure yet,' said Mum. 'It depends when Jamie comes back.'

'My birthday is two weeks away,' I said. 'Will I be home by then?'

Mum didn't answer.

While I was packing my suitcase, the doorbell rang.

I heard Zara answer the door and tell Kelly that Mum was too upset to come down.

'She sends her love,' said Zara. 'And says thank you for helping out.'

Kelly made understanding noises.

When I came down with my suitcase, Kelly gave me a big smile and a hug.

'Don't worry,' said Kelly. 'You'll be our little girl until your mother feels better.'

Our little girl.

It was such a warm feeling.

Before I left, Zara packed me another huge suitcase full of clothes.

'But I'm only staying for a few nights,' I said.

'With our mother,' said Zara, 'you never know.'

When we got to the Turner's house, Farrah came running downstairs to greet me.

'Hiiiiii!' said Farrah, in a really excited voice. 'Do you want to see my bedroom?'

It felt a little weird. Like, overly friendly.

I mean, Farrah pretty much ignored me at Lottie's party.

'You'll love it, Scarlett,' said Kelly. 'It's a girls' paradise up there. And you can show Farrah all the clothes you brought.'

'I don't even know what I have,' I said. 'Zara packed most of it.'

Farrah's bedroom was the pinkest room I'd ever seen. Pink walls, a pink carpet and pastel pink bed linen that smelt like fresh apples. There was an inflatable bed with a sleeping bag and pillow laid out for me under Farrah's cabin bed.

'I know it's a bit young,' said Farrah, in a slightly anxious voice. 'I mean, especially to someone from New York. I keep asking Mum to repaint it.'

'It looks really pretty,' I said. 'I love what you've done with the fairy lights.'

Farrah beamed. 'Put your suitcases by the bed,' she said. 'I'll show you the kitchen. You can get filtered water and ice cubes from the fridge. And I'm allowed a can of Coca Cola every day if I want. You can have one too.'

I gave Farrah a polite smile. Having Coca Cola isn't a big deal to me. We have loads of junk food and drink at home and there are no rules about when I can have it.

Farrah's house was small, compared to mine, but it felt a lot warmer and cosier. Everything was so tidy. And clean.

The whole house smelt of bleach and lemons. There was literally not one crumb or speck of dust anywhere, and Farrah's mother ran around constantly wiping, hoovering and polishing.

'My mum's a clean freak,' Farrah told me. 'She has germ phobia. She hates dirt.'

I was on best behaviour at dinner, smiling and saying thank you and clearing up after myself.

Kelly kept telling me what a nice girl I was and how pleased she was to have me over.

'Farrah could do with more friends like you,' Kelly told me, when I carried empty bowls and glasses into the kitchen. 'Lottie and Farrah had yet another falling out yesterday. Lottie was throwing her weight around as usual.'

'Why is Lottie so mean?' I asked. 'I don't get it.'

Kelly gave me big, sympathetic eyes. 'Well, hopefully, you and Farrah can have each other's backs from now on.'

At bedtime, Farrah tried to braid my hair, but she couldn't.

'Your hair is crazy knotty,' said Farrah.

'I know,' I said. 'But whenever I brush it, it just gets bigger.'

Kelly appeared in the doorway then, with hot chocolate and cookies on a tray. 'Frizzy hair needs special products, Scarlett,' she said. 'I'll buy you some when I'm next in town.'

'You really don't have to –'

'It would be my pleasure,' said Kelly. 'You're our little girl, right now.'

I smiled.

After that, we watched a movie on Farrah's laptop.

Kelly watched the movie with us too.

Farrah kept telling her mother to leave, but I liked Kelly being with us. It was amazing to think that a grown-up woman would actually want to spend time with her daughter.

When we got into bed, Kelly tucked the sleeping bag around me and told me the angels were keeping me safe.

It was heaven. Absolute heaven.

Farrah and I stayed up for a little while, singing songs from Grease and talking about dance moves.

As we were falling asleep, I asked Farrah about the Dolores Rush dance contest.

'How do you enter?' I asked.

'You go to the school office and fill in an application form,' said Farrah.

'And winners get a scholarship?' I asked. 'To Dolores's school in London?'

'Only the best solo dancer within a winning squad gets a scholarship,' said Farrah. 'That prize is like ... impossible. You basically have to win the whole contest. None of the girls at St Valentine's are interested in the scholarship, anyway. It's for a boarding school and it's so far away. We all just want to win the trophy and the cash prizes.'

'My sister lives in London,' I said. 'If I went to that school, I could see her at weekends. And I'd live with other girls all week. It would be like having a family.'

'You already have a family,' said Farrah.

I made a noise. Like, 'Mmm.'

'Look, I may as well tell you,' said Farrah. 'You can't enter the contest without a dance squad. And no one is going to join you and go up against Lottie.'

'Why not?' I asked.

'Well, for one thing, Lottie is a machine,' said Farrah. 'She trains day and night and studies the contest rules and previous winners. I mean, she knows that contest backwards. And also ... well, when people compete with

Lottie, they become her enemy. And nobody wants to be her enemy.'

'I think I'm already her enemy,' I said.

Farrah laughed. 'I like you, Scarlett. You're not scared of Lottie at all. You're either brave or crazy.'

'What are we going to do about the walk to school tomorrow?' I asked. 'I mean ... if Lottie doesn't want to walk with me.'

'It's fine,' said Farrah. 'Lottie is being a pain right now anyway. You and I will walk together, and Lottie can walk by herself.'

LOTTIE

I couldn't believe it.

Farrah didn't call for me this morning. She *always* calls for me on the way to school.

Honestly. We have one stupid argument at my sleepover, and now she's sulking. Talk about childish.

By the time I called for Primrose and Sophie they'd already left, so I ended up walking alone. Which made me furious. I was even more furious when I got to school and saw Farrah standing with Scarlett by *our* desk.

I pushed past Farrah and sat down without saying a word. Eventually, Scarlett went to sit with Amina, and Farrah sat down next to me.

'Hiiiii,' Farrah said, like nothing was wrong.

'Why didn't you call for me?' I asked, in a cold voice.

Farrah shrugged. 'It's not set in stone, is it? If you must know, I walked with Scarlett this morning. Scarlett stayed over at my *house* last night.'

That really threw me.

'Scarlett stayed over at your house?' I asked. 'Why?'

'Oh, just for a sleepover,' said Farrah. 'You know. We're getting really friendly now. It was fun, actually. No one bossed me around. Or made a big deal about pyjamas.'

'Oh my god, Farrah,' I said. 'What is your problem? I gave you the best bed at my sleepover *and* the best pyjamas. You can be such a princess sometimes.'

'Fine,' said Farrah. 'Call me a princess. I don't care. I'll just hang out with my *new* friend instead.'

She turned and gave Scarlett a big smile.

'If you want to hang out with show-offs, then forget about being on my dance squad,' I said. 'I only want girls who are dedicated.'

Farrah stiffened. 'Okay, okay,' she said. 'No need to have a hissy fit. I'm sorry, alright? I just didn't like the pyjamas.'

'That's no excuse for ditching me on the way to school,' I said. 'I had to walk alone. And I was nearly *late*.'

'Sorreeee Lottie,' said Farrah, in a pleading voice. 'Look, it wasn't my fault, okay? I didn't tell you before, because it's private and stuff. But Scarlett is staying at my house because her stepdad left and her mum is having a nervous breakdown.'

'No way,' I said. 'Scarlett's mother is having a nervous breakdown?'

Farrah nodded. 'It sounds really bad. Scarlett says she wants to move to London to live with her sister. She talked about winning the Dolores Rush Dance Contest. You know, to get a scholarship. Because she hates being at home so much.'

'Miss Miel will never choose her to go forward,' I said. 'She's only been here five minutes and she doesn't even have a squad. We've been practising for months.' I thought for a moment. 'Are you sure Scarlett's mother is having a nervous breakdown? I thought she was like some big shot talent agent or something.'

'Maybe not such a big shot after all,' said Farrah. We looked at each other. Then we laughed.

'How long is Scarlett staying with you?' I asked.

'I don't know.' Farrah looked awkward.

'Does that mean you'll be walking with Scarlett every morning until she leaves?' I asked.

'Well, yeah,' said Farrah. 'I can't exactly leave the house without her, can I? But we can call for you too.'

'Okay,' I said. 'Fine. But as soon as Scarlett goes home, it'll be just the A-Squad again. Deal?'

'Sure.' Farrah nodded. But she didn't quite meet my eye.

SCARLETT

After registration, we had science. I expected to sit on my own because we have to sit in pairs for science and the class is an odd number. But actually, I got lucky. Lottie had to leave for some official head girl duty, so Mr Swinny made Farrah and I sit together.

'Hey sleepover sister,' Farrah whispered, when I sat down beside her. 'Thank god I'm sitting with you today. Lottie's being a total nightmare.'

The science project was about bees and how much weight they can carry on their legs. It turns out bees can carry around 35% of their body weight in pollen.

Farrah kept joking about Mr Swinny carrying more than 35% of his body weight because he's sort of overweight. I felt bad laughing, because Mr Swinny seems nice, but it was pretty funny.

Amina kept shushing us. To be honest, it was a little bit

annoying. I can see why Farrah calls Amina 'policewoman Jones.'

Farrah even drew a picture of Amina dressed as a police officer, blowing a whistle. Underneath it she wrote:

'Stand down, Officer Jones, put your whistle away.'

It was really hard not to laugh because the picture looked so much like Amina. Farrah had drawn Amina wearing an oversized girl guide uniform, eyes bulging, long, black braid over her shoulder. She'd got Amina's expression just right – like a nervous teacher. And she'd even tucked a copy of *Lord of the Rings* under Amina's skinny, cartoon arm.

As part of the science lesson, we had to weigh ourselves so we could measure 35% of our own body weight.

Farrah was the heaviest girl in class.

Truthfully, Farrah is bigger than most girls our age. She's sort of sturdy and grown-up looking, you know? Like she could be three years older than the rest of us. But it's not as if she's unattractive. She has a cute face, shiny blonde hair and sparkling blue eyes. Very angelic.

I could tell Farrah felt bad about being the heaviest, even though she acted like it was no big deal.

'Tall girls always weigh more,' I told her. 'Olympic athletes are heavy. It's all height and muscle. Don't worry about it. I weigh nearly as much as my big sister because I'm tall and strong. Weight doesn't mean anything.'

Farrah looked at me for a long time. Then she said: 'Wow. You're nice. If I was doing this experiment with Lottie, she'd be boasting about how little she weighs.'

'Who wants to be teeny tiny?' I asked. 'All the models and athletes are tall.'

Farrah looked happy when I said that.

Later in the lesson, Lottie came back. You could tell she

was annoyed that Farrah and I were working together, especially when Mr Swinny made Lottie join our group as a third wheel.

Lottie got busy right away, rewriting our report in neater handwriting.

Farrah rolled her eyes and whispered, 'Sooo typical of Little Miss Perfect.'

At break time, Farrah went off to dance with Lottie and the 'A-Squad'. I don't get how Farrah can dislike Lottie one minute, and be dancing with her the next.

While Farrah was dancing, I went to the school office to find out about dance contest applications.

Mrs Brawn was behind the glass office window, frowning at paperwork.

'Excuse me,' I said. 'Do you have forms for the Dolores Rush Dance Contest?'

Mrs Brawn didn't look up. Her clipped, grey hair bobbed up and down as she flipped pages. 'You're too late to put yourself forward for that,' she said. 'The contest is next month.'

'Has the school already picked a squad to go forward?' I asked.

'No one has been *officially* chosen,' said Mrs Brawn, sounding irritated. 'That's another lot of paperwork for me to fill out. But Miss Miel will put forward Lottie Collins's dance squad a few weeks before the contest. She does every year.'

'So there's still time to enter?' I asked.

Mrs Brawn's head snapped up. 'Do you have a dance squad?'

'Um ... not yet,' I admitted. 'I've only just found out about the contest. But I'm hoping to find –'

'You can't enter without a squad,' said Mrs Brawn, looking back down at her paperwork.

'But ... I can still enter?' I asked. 'I mean, you haven't made your final choice?'

'There is no final choice,' snapped Mrs Brawn. 'Lottie Collins's squad is the only entry. It's just a question of putting their details on the final form –'

'Which you haven't done yet?'

'The final form isn't even online,' said Mrs Brawn. 'It won't be available until a week before the contest. Now if you don't mind, I'm busy.'

'Thank you for your time,' I said.

Mrs Brawn made an exasperated sound. Then she pulled a black curtain across the glass.

LOTTIE

For the rest of the week, Scarlett tagged along with us on the way to school.

It was so annoying.

Okay, so Scarlett is having a family crisis, but why is she staying with *my* best friend? Why not Amina? Amina picks up all the stray dogs. Like Marianne. No one spoke to Marianne until Amina took her in.

You can tell Farrah thinks Scarlett is really cool, which is even more annoying. Why can't Farrah see what a show-off Scarlett is? All Scarlett does is go on about New York and all the 'great' dance classes she did there.

'I did tap and street dance and break dancing.'

Ugh.

I should get Scarlett a t-shirt made that says: 'I'm so pretty and talented'.

Okay, so Scarlett never exactly says those words. But that's what she means.

Farrah's family are sort of flashy. They're into brand names and expensive cars and that kind of thing. So it's typical that Farrah would be all over a girl like Scarlett, because Scarlett has a big house and a swimming pool.

I can't wait for Scarlett to go home and everything to go back to normal. In the meantime, I just try to ignore her.

SCARLETT

I had the most amazing week at Farrah's house.

Kelly made home-cooked meals and washed our clothes and helped with homework. In the evenings, the whole family ate together and Kelly asked questions about our day.

Kelly and Doug kept saying I must miss my family and my 'great big' house. Which was funny.

What family?

On Friday after school, Kelly said she had a surprise for me: hair products that worked like magic potions on frizzy hair.

After washing my hair with special shampoo and conditioner, Kelly added this serum stuff and scrunched my hair into curls.

My hair went from a dry, frizzy mess to gleaming, separated waves. I couldn't believe the difference, especially when Farrah princess-braided my hair and 'styled me up' in one of the outfits Zara had packed for me.

Twirling around in skinny jeans, sequin baseball boots, a green sweater and a chunky, amber bangle, I felt like a princess.

'Wow, Scarlett,' said Farrah. 'You look like a fashion model.'

'My goodness,' Kelly smiled. 'You really are your mother's daughter.'

'I hope not,' I said.

On Saturday afternoon, Farrah suggested we go to the pizza park together.

Kelly gave us cash to buy food and cold drinks.

'You don't have to get pizza, Scarlett,' Kelly told me. 'I know everyone calls it the pizza park, but they sell hot dogs and burgers too.'

'Aren't you coming with us?' I asked.

Farrah gave a loud laugh. 'Why do you want my mother around all the time?'

'Why *don't* you want your mother around?' I challenged. 'She's really cool.'

Kelly gave a whoop of laughter. 'See, Farrah? I *am* cool. But I won't cramp your style. You girls go and have fun by yourself.'

When Farrah and I arrived at the park, lots of girls from school were there, hanging out by the food vans, paddling in the boating lake and eating ice creams.

Everyone stared at me, but this time I felt like it was for the right reasons. I was wearing a polka dot dress with cork sandals, and my hair gleamed in bouncy, red waves.

'Look.' Farrah pointed. 'There's Lottie and the girls.'

Lottie, Primrose and Sophie were dancing on one of the many green lawns.

'Oh my god,' said Farrah. 'They're dancing *again*. I am so bored of dance contest practice. Lottie is like Hitler. She wants everything to be *perfect*.'

When the girls saw us coming towards them, they stopped dancing and stared.

'Wow, Scarlett,' said Primrose. 'You look amazing.'

Sophie nodded and nodded.

Lottie didn't say anything.

'What are you guys up to?' Farrah asked.

'A-Squad dance practice,' said Lottie. 'But I guess we need to stop if *she's* here.' Lottie jerked a thumb at me.

'Why don't we perform Grease?' said Primrose, doing a spin, nearly falling over, then laughing at herself.

'Great idea,' said Farrah.

'Sorry,' said Lottie. 'There aren't enough parts for everyone. Scarlett will just have to sit it out.'

'Don't be stupid,' Farrah laughed. 'Grease has loads of parts. Sandy, Danny, Rizzo, Rizzo's boyfriend –'

'Kenickie,' I said, helpfully.

'I should be Sandy,' said Farrah.

'You're always Sandy,' said Lottie. 'Sophie should have a chance at playing her for once. She asked last time. Remember?'

'Sandy is totally wrong for you, Sophie,' said Farrah. 'I should be Sandy. I'm blonde.'

'No, *Sophie* should play Sandy,' said Lottie. 'It's her turn. You can't come along with your new friend and push us all around.'

Sophie looked really nervous. She fiddled with her brown, princess curls like she wished they were blonde.

'What do you think, Scarlett?' said Farrah. 'You're from New York. You know all about the movie business.'

Truthfully, New York is much more about television and theatre than the movies, but ...

'Farrah should be Sandy,' I said. 'She's perfect.'

Lottie looked absolutely furious. 'Oh my *god*, Scarlett.

Who do you think you are? Why don't you go back to New York where you belong?'

Farrah gasped. 'That's *racist*, Lottie.'

'It's not racist,' said Lottie. 'New York isn't a *race*.' She turned to Sophie. 'You agree with me, don't you? You should play Sandy.'

Sophie tensed up, obviously hating being stuck in the middle.

Nobody said anything.

'Oh, do what you like.' Lottie marched off towards the boating lake.

'I think she's really angry,' said Sophie, sounding nervous. 'You should go after her, Farrah. Say you're sorry.'

'I'm sick of running around after Lottie,' said Farrah. 'Let's just hang out without her.'

'But she'll be *furious*,' said Sophie.

'So what?' said Farrah. 'Lottie was really rude to Scarlett just now. She needs to apologise. If she can't do that ... well, let her sulk.'

We spent the rest of the afternoon singing and performing in the park. I taught everyone a really cool dance routine for 'We'll Always Be Together'. Then we got wood-fired pizza and ate it straight from the box, sitting on the grass.

'You're such a great dancer, Scarlett,' said Sophie, wrestling with her hot pizza. 'I wish you were on our dance squad.'

'Me too,' I said. 'I'm desperate to enter the Dolores Rush Dance Contest. I want that scholarship more than anything. And it sounds like your squad always gets chosen to go forward.'

'Lottie would never let you join us,' said Sophie. 'It's a real shame too because you could bring so much to our routine. We've never won the contest before. I bet with you, we'd have a better chance.'

'How come Lottie has the final say in all this?' I asked.

'Because she's the bossiest,' said Primrose.

'Bossy is right,' said Farrah. 'She tells everyone what to do.'

'Aren't you three old enough to think for yourselves?' I asked.

Sophie gave a nervous laugh.

When we'd finished our pizza, we all went back to Farrah's house to mess around with clothes and make-up.

Sophie mixed my clothes to make new styles and gave me fashion tips.

'You need to remember less is more,' said Sophie. 'Only wear one bright colour. Everything else should be neutral. And one bold accessory.'

While we were dressing up and having fun, Zara called.

I grabbed my phone and hurried downstairs.

'What is it?' I whispered. 'Is Mum okay?'

'She's fine,' said Zara. 'She and Jamie just got back together.'

'Oh.' I let the news sink in. 'Well, that's good, isn't it?'

'No, it's not good,' said Zara. 'Jamie has been seeing someone else. A twenty-six-year-old girl he met at work. Mum found out from one of Jamie's friends, but she's still taking him back. Why does she let men treat her like this?'

'I don't know,' I said.

'I'm just phoning to warn you,' said Zara. 'Mum wants you home tomorrow. She doesn't want you to outstay your welcome with the Turners.'

'I don't want to go home,' I said. 'I want to live with you in London.'

'We've talked about this,' said Zara. 'Your school –'

'There's a dance contest coming up,' I said. 'I could win a scholarship in London. I just need to find some girls to dance with me.'

'It's good to dream,' said Zara. 'Keep on dreaming.'

LOTTIE

Scarlett ruined my weekend.

Totally ruined it.

Who does she think she is, trying to barge her way into my friendship group?

'Ooo, I'm Scarlett, I know about the movie business.'

And Farrah, bringing Scarlett over without asking, then trying to boss me around. Totally out of line.

I didn't wait for Farrah this morning. I was way too angry to walk with her, so I left super early and called for Primrose and Sophie alone.

'Where's Farrah?' Primrose asked, when I knocked on her door.

I shrugged. 'Probably walking with Scarlett. I don't know. Those two really got on my nerves over the weekend.'

Primrose looked awkward.

When we got to Sophie's house, Sophie asked the same question.

'Where's Farrah?'

'I don't know,' I said. 'I'm not her keeper. I don't really care about Farrah right now. Not until she apologises.'

Sophie gave me a sympathetic nod. She goes along with anything to stop an argument. I never really know if she agrees with me or not.

When we got to school, I sat in my usual seat and waited for Farrah to arrive. She came in with Scarlett, which made me even angrier.

'Hey,' said Farrah, sitting down beside me. 'What's up? Why did you leave without me?'

I shrugged and didn't answer.

Farrah kept asking if I was okay and trying to make jokes, like nothing was wrong. I ignored her.

At break time, I told Primrose and Sophie that we were going to rehearse outside.

'The dance studio is really stuffy in this weather,' I said. 'We need some fresh air.'

'What about Farrah?' asked Primrose. 'She won't know where we're going.'

'Farrah wants to be with Scarlett right now,' I said. 'I think we should leave her to it. And just get really good at dancing as a three. The dance contest isn't far away. We can't afford to have someone in the squad who keeps missing practice.'

'Farrah only missed one practice,' Primrose pointed out.

'No,' I said. 'Farrah missed this Saturday too.'

'But we never usually practise on Saturday,' said Primrose. 'How could Farrah have known?'

'She should have guessed,' I said. 'I mean, the contest is a month away. But she was too busy hanging out with show-off Scarlett to care.'

Primrose and Sophie didn't say anything.

'Come on,' I said, and marched them out to the nature area to practise our routine.

About halfway through break time, Farrah appeared.

'What are you doing *here*?' Farrah demanded. 'Why did you sneak off without telling me?'

'I thought you'd be hanging out with Scarlett,' I said. 'Like you have been all week. Look, Farrah, maybe there's no room for you in the squad if you're going to be so unreliable.'

Farrah looked like I'd stabbed her in the heart. Then her eyes hardened.

'Fine,' she said. 'Be like that.' And she stormed off.

To be honest, I didn't expect Farrah to take me so seriously. I mean, I said *maybe* there was no room for her in the squad. But if she wants to overreact, that's up to her.

Farrah will come back in the end. She always does.

SCARLETT

It felt really weird going back home.

Mum and Jamie were all icky and lovey-dovey with each other, so I spent most of Sunday in my bedroom, staying out of their way.

On Monday morning, Farrah called for me on her way to school.

I was surprised, but happy.

'Where's Lottie?' I asked. 'Don't you usually call for her?'

'I did,' said Farrah. 'She'd already left. I think she's in a mood about the pizza park. You'll look after me at school, won't you, Scarlett? Lottie is scary when she's angry.'

'Of course,' I said. 'We're sleepover sisters.'

Farrah complained about Lottie all the way to school. Then, when we arrived at school, she sat in her usual seat next to Little Miss Perfect.

I didn't get it. Why complain about Lottie, then hang around with her? And where did I fit in? Were Farrah and I friends or not?

At break time, it was even more confusing. I was doing sudoku puzzles with Amina and Marianne, when Farrah came running over looking really upset.

'Lottie just threw me out of her dance squad,' said

Farrah, leaning over to catch her breath. 'She's totally leaving me out on purpose. Just because I stood up to her.'

'You leave people out too, Farrah,' said Amina. 'With all your A-Squad dancing rubbish. You do it all the time.'

Farrah looked at Amina like she was something disgusting. Then she took my arm and walked me across the playground.

'You understand, don't you Scarlett?' said Farrah. 'You know what Lottie's like.'

'Definitely,' I said. 'Lottie is really mean. I don't get why everyone loves her so much. She's not even fun to be around.'

'Lottie didn't used to be so bad,' said Farrah. 'But she's been so stressy lately. Probably because of her glasses.'

'What glasses?' I asked.

Farrah gave a smug nod. 'Lottie needs glasses *all* the time. Her sister told us.'

'So why doesn't she wear them?' I asked.

'Because she has to be perfect,' said Farrah. 'Especially while she's dancing. You have to admit, it would look pretty weird dancing with glasses on.'

'I knew a dancer in New York who wore glasses,' I said. 'She looked great.'

'Whatever,' said Farrah. 'It's not the point. Lottie should be setting an example to the rest of us, not lying to her parents.'

'Well, why don't you tell her parents?' I said. 'If it bothers you so much.'

'Are you kidding me?' Farrah's eyes widened. 'Lottie would kill me.'

We both looked at each other.

'I dare you to do it, Scarlett,' said Farrah. 'Go round to

Lottie's house tonight and tell her parents she doesn't wear her glasses at school.'

'No way,' I said. 'I'm not a telltale.'

'Suit yourself.' Farrah shrugged. 'I mean, I thought you were like, this New York tough girl. But if you're afraid ...'

'I'm not afraid.'

'Then prove it,' said Farrah.

I felt a spark of fear in my stomach, like when I'm about to go on a rollercoaster. Scared, but excited, you know? Because it *would* serve Lottie right to get into trouble. Also, I didn't want Farrah to think I was afraid, because I wasn't.

'Okay,' I told Farrah. 'I'll do it.'

Farrah gave a whoop. 'Call me as soon as you do it, okay? I want to hear everything.'

After school that day, I walked to Lottie's house. When I knocked on the front door, there was a long silence. At first, I thought no one would answer and I was off the hook. Honestly, I was starting to feel uncertain about the whole idea. Then a tall, blonde girl in grey sweats opened the door.

I guessed the girl was Lottie's sister because she had the same pointed nose and pale skin. But she was really tall, with thick, blonde hair, whereas Lottie is tiny and has shiny, brown hair.

The tall girl smiled. 'You must be one of Lottie's friends. I love that *dress*. Yellow looks really good on you. Probably because of your beautiful, red hair.'

'Thanks.' I touched my curls and gave an awkward smile. No one had ever called my hair beautiful before. It felt weird but good.

We smiled at each other, and I wondered how Lottie's sister could be so nice when Lottie was such a nightmare.

Lottie's sister turned to the house. 'Lottie! Someone at the door for you.' Then she disappeared back inside.

A moment later, Lottie came to the door. She was eating an orange ice lolly and wearing glasses.

I stared at her. She stared at me. Then Lottie whipped off her glasses.

'What are *you* doing here?' Lottie demanded, in a really unfriendly voice.

'I need to talk to your mother about something,' I said.

'About what?' Lottie demanded.

I put on a really serious voice then, and said: 'About your glasses.'

At that exact minute, Lottie's mother came into the hallway.

'Oh! Hello, Scarlett,' said Mrs Collins. 'Love the hair. I can tell you've been staying with the Turners. You look like you've had a makeover.'

I put on my best smile and said: 'Hello, Mrs Collins. How are you?'

Mrs Collins gave me worried eyes. 'I heard about your mother. I really am sorry –'

'It's okay,' I said. 'Jamie's come back now.'

'Right.' Mrs Collins nodded. 'Well ... I suppose you're here to see Lottie. Would you like a *homemade* orange ice lolly?'

It was funny the way Lottie's Mum said the words *homemade* like she was really proud.

'No thanks,' I said.

'Are you sure?' Mrs Collins clearly thought I was crazy for not wanting an ice lolly. I often get that with parents. But I can have ice lollies, candy and ice cream whenever I want. It's not a big deal for me.

'Actually, Mrs Collins,' I said. 'I need to talk to you

about Lottie. She hasn't been wearing her glasses at school and I thought you should know.'

My heart was absolutely racing in my chest. Telling on Lottie seemed hilarious when Farrah and I talked about it. But in the moment, I felt sort of mean.

Lottie turned bright red. 'You are SUCH a liar! I wear my glasses *all* the time!'

That really annoyed me. I mean, yes, I understand that Lottie was upset. But she didn't need to call me a liar.

'You don't wear them, Lottie,' I said. 'I've never once seen you wear them.'

'How would you know?' said Lottie. 'We're not even friends. I don't like you. Nobody likes you. Farrah only hung out with you because your mum was having some kind of nervous breakdown.'

'Lottie!' said Mrs Collins.

'Sorry,' said Lottie. 'But it's true.'

'Do you know what else is true?' I said. 'You don't wear your glasses at school.' I turned to Mrs Collins. 'You can ask anyone. You can even ask Mrs Singh. She'll tell you.'

Mrs Collins put her hands on her hips. 'Lottie, those glasses are to help your eyesight. Look, I know they're not very cool –'

'Mum, will you SHUT UP!' Lottie roared. Then she went stomping inside the house and upstairs.

Mrs Collins looked embarrassed. 'This all sounds like one big misunderstanding. Look, I really don't know what to believe.'

'I'm telling you the truth,' I said. 'Lottie doesn't wear her glasses. I'd better go. Mum is waiting for me.'

That was a lie, but I wanted to get off that doorstep as soon as possible. By the time I got home, I felt really bad. I wasn't sure I'd done the right thing. In fact, I was pretty sure I'd just started a load of trouble.

I called Farrah and told her what happened.

'Oh my god,' said Farrah. 'Lottie should wear her glasses. It's her who's in the wrong, not us. Why should the rules apply to everyone else and not her?'

I didn't say anything. But I really wasn't looking forward to going to school the next day.

LOTTIE

I was so furious.

I couldn't believe Scarlett could do something so sneaky and mean. To actually turn up on my doorstep and tell Mum about my glasses.

It was absolutely unforgivable.

After Scarlett left, I stayed in my bedroom stewing over what had happened. Someone must have told Scarlett about my glasses, and I knew exactly who.

Farrah.

After an hour or so of sulking, I came downstairs and called Farrah. She didn't answer her phone, so I called five more times. When Farrah finally picked up, she sounded really cautious.

'Hello?'

'Thanks a lot, Farrah,' I said.

'I don't know what you're talking about,' said Farrah, in that airy way she does when she's definitely lying.

I couldn't shout at Farrah about the glasses thing, because Mum was listening in.

'Forget about being in my dance squad ever again,' I hissed. Then I hung up.

'Oh love,' said Mum. 'That was a bit much. Phone back and apologise.'

'No way,' I said. 'If Farrah wants to go off with the new girl, then I'm not waiting around. We're finished.'

Cassandra came bounding up the stairs then, giant headphones around her neck. 'What's with all the shouting?'

'The new girl is trying to steal my best friend,' I said.

'I know how we can make things better,' said Mum. 'How about I take you and Farrah shopping at the weekend? We can get an ice cream afterwards and you two can settle your differences. I've been meaning to catch up with Kelly for a while.'

'I don't want to see Farrah ever again,' I said.

'Oh, don't be silly,' said Mum. 'You won't feel that way by the weekend. I'll set something up.'

I felt a bit better then. I was still angry with Farrah, but now Mum was on my side I knew it would get sorted out.

'Really, Mum?' said Cassandra. 'Do you think this is good parenting? Shouldn't Lottie handle this herself?'

'What?' Mum pretended to look innocent. 'I'm just taking my little girl and her friend for an ice cream.' She winked at me. 'We might not be able to compete with the big house, but we have other talents.'

'Friendships aren't about competing,' said Cassandra. 'If you have to win a friendship, you've already lost.'

I ignored Cassandra and her ultra-mature comments. As far as I was concerned, it was all settled. Mum would take Farrah and me on a shopping trip, and we'd make friends again.

I'd ignore Farrah all week, of course, just to make my point. If she wants to hang out with Scarlett, well ... then she can't hang out with the A-Squad.

Sometimes, people have to make a choice. I know Farrah will choose us in the end.

SCARLETT

The next day, Farrah called for me again.

'Hey sleepover sister,' she said, in this really high, excited voice. 'Do you want to walk to school again today?'

'Sure,' I said. 'Where's Lottie?'

'Oh, she's still angry with me,' said Farrah. 'She called me a hundred times last night. She was all like, *we will never be friends ever again.* So stupid. I mean, all I did was tell you about her glasses.'

'It was me who went to her house,' I said. 'What was she yelling at you for?'

'I don't know,' said Farrah. 'She was being a total idiot.'

When we arrived at school, Lottie was sitting upright at her desk, wearing her glasses. Typical Lottie – the glasses looked pretty good. They suited her neat young lady style and made her nose look all pointy and cute.

'Hey,' Farrah whispered. 'Check out perfect Lottie's nerd glasses.'

I let out a spurt of laughter. It was just so funny to insult someone as dignified as Lottie.

Lottie turned around then and looked ... uncertain. Then she crossed her arms and turned her whole body away.

Farrah grabbed my arm. 'Oh my god. Please sit with me, Scarlett. Lottie is totally ignoring me again.'

'Of course,' I said. 'Where do you want to sit?'

Farrah pointed to a spare desk beside Scarlett, and we sat together.

Lottie looked really startled when she saw us do that.

She sort of tensed up and kept sneaking looks at Farrah and me.

After registration, we had Geography.

Normally, Lottie and Farrah sit together in Geography, but today, Farrah sat with me.

Lottie grabbed a spare chair and wedged it onto Primrose and Sophie's desk. The girls moved aside for her, but you could see they weren't happy about it.

Then Mr Nowak came in and told Lottie to move.

'There's no space for you there, Charlotte,' he said. 'Take the desk at the front, please.'

So Lottie had to sit by herself again.

At break time, Lottie went off with Primrose and Sophie to the dance studio. I was about to find Amina and Marianne, when Farrah grabbed my arm.

'Hey, sleepover sister,' she said. 'Will you teach me some of those really cool breakdance moves?'

'Sure,' I said. 'Amina and Marianne won't mind. They want to play chess and I'm not at their level.'

'Great,' said Farrah. 'Let's go to the dance studio.'

'But that's where Lottie goes,' I said. 'Why don't we go somewhere else?'

'Why should we go somewhere else?' said Farrah. 'The dance studio has the best surface. And it's for everyone, not just Little Miss Perfect.'

When we got to the dance studio, Lottie and the other girls were there.

'What are you two doing here?' Lottie snapped.

'Dancing,' said Farrah.

'Well, we were here first,' said Lottie. 'Go somewhere else.'

'Why don't *you* go somewhere else?' said Farrah. 'You're here every day. It's our turn.' She looked at me. 'Right?'

'You don't own the dance studio, Lottie,' I said. 'We're allowed to practise here.'

'Exactly,' said Farrah, holding down a smirk. 'We don't think you should be dancing with glasses, anyway. Not unless you get a piece of elastic to hold them on.'

Lottie went bright red. 'You're teasing me about my glasses.'

'I'm so *not*,' said Farrah. 'I was just worried those glasses might be dangerous. I mean they're so *big*.'

Primrose sniggered.

'Shut up, Farrah,' said Lottie.

'Don't talk to me like that,' said Farrah. 'You're being a total bully.'

'No, you and Scarlett are the bullies,' said Lottie. 'Just wait until Mrs Singh hears about this.' She spun around and stalked off.

We all stood in silence for a moment.

Then Sophie said, 'Is she going to tell on us?'

'Of course she won't,' said Farrah. 'If she does, Mrs Singh will tell *her* off for time-wasting. Hey, do you guys want to dance with us now Lottie's gone?'

'Okay,' said Sophie.

Primrose nodded.

We made up a super-cool dance routine with breakdance moves thrown in. Primrose and Sophie were really sweet, asking me lots of questions about dancing in New York.

When the bell rang, we headed into school for English.

Farrah grabbed my arm as we neared the classroom. 'You'll sit with me, won't you? You have to protect me from Lottie's evil eyes. I think she's trying to shoot lasers through her glasses.'

We both laughed.

Lottie was already in class at her usual desk – the one she and Farrah usually sit at together. She was frowning at a copy of *To Kill a Mockingbird.*

Farrah and I walked right past Lottie, then Farrah giggled, grabbed my arm and pulled me to sit at the desk behind her.

While Farrah and I were taking turns to read *To Kill a Mockingbird*, Lottie kept checking her reflection in the window and adjusting her glasses.

Farrah whispered: 'Hey, look at Lottie, checking herself out. Talk about self-obsessed.'

Lottie turned around then. 'What did you say?'

'Nothing,' said Farrah, in an innocent voice.

When Lottie turned back around, Farrah whispered: 'She looks like an angry librarian.'

Farrah and I burst out laughing. I didn't mean to laugh, but it was just so funny. Lottie really did look ridiculous.

'Girls,' said Miss Matthews. 'Will you keep it down?'

Lottie put her hand up then. 'They're laughing at me, Miss Matthews. Because of my glasses.'

'We're totally not,' said Farrah. 'Lottie thinks the world revolves around her and her glasses.'

'Surely no one would laugh about glasses,' said Miss Matthews. 'I think glasses make you look very intelligent.'

Which is probably the worst thing Miss Matthews could have said, because she wears glasses too, and nobody wants to be like the teacher.

Towards the end of English, Lottie took her glasses off and put them in her pencil case. Then she asked to sit closer to the board.

'Isn't that what your glasses are for?' said Miss Matthews. 'So you can see the board better?'

'I don't have to wear them all the time,' said Lottie. 'Only if I feel like it.'

'That's not what your sister told us,' Farrah shouted. 'You have to wear them *all* the time.'

Lottie turned around then and gave us the most poisonous look.

Farrah and I both looked at each other, then burst out laughing.

LOTTIE

I didn't wear my glasses to school after that.

Obviously.

I'm not an idiot. There was no way I was making myself an easy target.

The rest of the week was pretty horrible. I had to sit alone during registration, and I felt so exposed. Like everyone was staring at me and whispering.

Primrose and Sophie still danced with me at break and lunch, but they kept looking at Scarlett and Farrah, who were dancing in the same space.

I nearly said to them: 'Why don't you dance with those two? If you love them so much.' But I didn't, because I had a horrible feeling that they actually might.

On Friday night, Mum reminded me about the shopping trip with Farrah and Kelly the next day.

'You can buy some new clothes to go with your glasses,' said Mum. 'Farrah can help you. She's a good shopper. Just like her mother.'

'I don't want to go shopping with Farrah,' I said. 'Can't we cancel it?'

'Why on earth would we do that?' asked Mum. 'It's been arranged all week. And you love shopping and ice cream.'

'Farrah's been really mean this week,' I said. 'She keeps ganging up on me. She's the last person I want to see me in glasses.'

'But everyone sees you in glasses at school,' said Mum.

I went quiet then, because of course, I hadn't been wearing my glasses very much.

'Charlotte, those glasses are to correct your eyesight,' said Mum, in a very careful voice. 'The optician told you to wear them all the time. If I find out you haven't been wearing them, there will be trouble.'

'I *have* been wearing them,' I said, in a flouncy voice. 'Fine. Whatever. I'll go shopping with Farrah and it'll be a nightmare. Thanks a lot.'

On Saturday, Kelly and Farrah pulled up outside our house in their big Range Rover.

Kelly gave me a cheery hello when I climbed into the car, but Farrah didn't say a word.

As we drove towards town, Farrah said: 'Oh, you're wearing your glasses.'

Not, 'nice glasses', or 'they really suit you' or anything like that.

'Yes,' I said, giving Farrah a look. 'Of course I am. You know I have to wear them.'

After that, Farrah and I didn't speak at all – even when we were clothes shopping.

Farrah got loads of new clothes, but I didn't get anything. Nothing looked right with my glasses.

'What's wrong with you, Lottie?' said Farrah. 'Why are you acting so stuck up?'

'Me?' I said. 'I think you're talking about your new friend. The one who thinks she's so above everyone.'

'At least Scarlett doesn't try to boss everyone around all the time,' said Farrah. 'And she's not a *baby*. She has her own phone. She doesn't have to use her *father's*.'

That made me so angry. I threw all my clothes on the floor and stormed out of the changing room.

Mum said, 'Uh oh. I'm seeing some teenage hormones.' She and Kelly gave each other this really patronising, knowing smile.

Ugh.

It was bad enough having the girls at school laugh at me. But now my own mother.

After that, I was sulky all day.

Mum kept telling me to cheer up and stop being such a misery, but I just couldn't.

And worse, every time we passed a shop mirror, I saw myself in the glasses and wanted to cry.

When we got home, I screamed my head off at Mum.

'How could you laugh at me like that with Farrah's Mum? You are SO RUDE.' Then I stomped up to my bedroom and cried on my bed. I tried to do it quietly, but Cassandra knocked on my door and asked what was wrong.

'NOTHING,' I screamed.

'Fine,' said Cassandra. 'I'll leave you alone if you're going to be like that. But Lottie – whatever you're going through, I've been there and worse.'

I didn't believe her.

My perfect big sister has no idea what I'm going through. She's never had to wear glasses or deal with a new girl stealing her best friend. She has no clue, just like Mum. No clue at all.

SCARLETT

Being at home is so weird right now.

Mum and Jamie are back together, but no one is talking about why Jamie left or where he went.

Mum walks around with this fake, bright smile on her face, pretending everything is fine. It's so stupid. Like she didn't spend days in bed crying.

Zara is back home too because she thinks I need support. I appreciate it, but she looks as unhappy as me.

We're all totally stuck in this horrible, awkward atmosphere.

No one has said it out loud, but certain conversations are off-limits. We can't talk about where Jamie went last week. And we can't ask Mum how she's feeling, because she's pretending to be happy, with shiny eyes and this super perky voice.

Jamie obviously feels bad about leaving, because he's being extra nice to everyone. But he's sort of *too* nice, you know? It's all fake.

Take this evening, for example.

Jamie asked if I wanted a birthday party. Like he was my real dad or something.

'Your birthday is next Saturday, right Scarlett?' Jamie enthused. 'Shall we throw you a super-duper party?'

Zara gave me a wink, like, take advantage if Jamie's going to be an idiot. And I thought, why not?

'I'd love to have a party,' I said. 'Can we get the pool cleaned?'

'Sure!' said Jamie.

'Really?' I said. 'You'll get the pool cleaned by next week?'

Mum gave Jamie a tense look. 'Next week is very busy

for me.'

Jamie laughed. 'Well, she's your daughter, sweetheart. And it is her birthday.'

Mum gave Jamie an icy smile. 'What would we do without you, darling?'

Ugh.

Mum runs her own talent agency and has five people working for her. But she's pathetic around Jamie right now.

Later that evening, I called Dad and told him about my birthday party.

'That's great, honey,' he said. 'I wish I could be there.'

'Will you come?' I asked. 'Please, please, PLEASE? Remember last year, you said you'd DEFINITELY come to my next birthday party.'

Dad laughed. 'Scarlett, we don't even live in the same country –'

'But you promised,' I said. 'You're always breaking promises.'

I let that one hang heavy.

'Okay, okay.' I could almost see Dad holding his hands up. 'I'll come. Just let me work out the flight arrangements.'

I gave a little squeal of excitement.

After I talked to Dad, I called Farrah and told her about the party.

'I'm going to invite the whole class,' I said. 'Even Lottie. Then maybe she'll forgive me for telling on her about the glasses.'

'Don't invite the whole class,' said Farrah. 'Haven't you learned your lesson? If you invite everyone, you look desperate. Invite like, half the class. And definitely don't invite Lottie. If you do that, she'll think you're apologising.'

'I'm not apologising,' I said. 'I'm just trying to make peace.'

'Yeah, Lottie won't get it,' said Farrah. 'She'll take it as a sign of weakness.'

'Okay,' I said. 'Fine. I won't invite Lottie. What about Primrose and Sophie. Should I invite them?'

'Definitely,' said Farrah. 'Call them up and ask them in person. That way, they can't say no.'

'Why would they say no?' I asked.

'Because they don't want to make Lottie angry,' Farrah explained. 'But they won't say no if you ask in person. It's too much pressure.'

I took Farrah's advice and phoned Primrose and Sophie. They both sounded really happy to be invited.

Sophie asked about dress codes and themes.

'I'll let you know, okay?' I said.

Primrose didn't ask about dress codes, but she did ask about dancing.

'I've been practising the moves you taught me,' she said. 'Can I show you tomorrow at break time?'

'Sure,' I said. 'But ... I mean, don't you usually dance with Lottie at break time? Won't she be annoyed with you?'

Long pause.

'Um ...' said Primrose. 'Sophie and I were thinking ... maybe we should dance with you and Farrah sometimes. We don't want to take sides between you and Lottie. So we think it's fair to split our time between you. And ... well, we thought we could make a squad with you too. So you could put yourself forward for the contest.'

'No way!' I felt a lifting in my chest. 'Really? You'd make a squad with me?'

'Of course,' said Primrose. 'Sophie and I even thought of a name for the squad. The Dream Team.'

'The Dream Team?' I laughed. 'I love it!'

Truthfully, I would have loved anything Primrose said at that moment. I was so excited.

'Of course, Miss Miel might not pick you to go forward for the contest,' said Primrose. 'But you never know. We've never won it with Lottie.' There was a long silence. Then Primrose added: 'Lottie's going to be furious, but fair's fair. Sophie and I have to do what's right.'

LOTTIE

I only meant to leave Farrah out of the dance squad for a few days, but after she and Scarlett started dancing together – well, I thought I'd leave her dangling a bit longer.

That was a big mistake, because today, Primrose and Sophie danced with Farrah and Scarlett.

I don't know how Scarlett managed to steal *all* my dancers. Why are my friends suddenly obsessed with her, like she's a celebrity? It doesn't make any sense.

It was so humiliating at break time. I went to the dance studio as usual, and there they were – Farrah, Scarlett, Primrose and Sophie, all dancing together.

At first, I thought Primrose and Sophie were just messing around while they waited for me. Which still felt bad. But then Farrah said: 'What are you doing here, Lottie? It's our turn with Primrose and Sophie today.'

'What are you talking about?' I asked.

'Primrose and Sophie have decided to split their time between us,' said Scarlett. 'They think it's the fair thing to do, now you and Farrah aren't getting along.'

Primrose and Sophie hung their heads and wouldn't meet my eye.

'But you signed up to *my* dance squad,' I told them. 'The A-Squad. I even made you certificates.'

'We're stuck in the middle,' said Primrose. 'We don't want to take sides. And Scarlett wants to enter the contest too.'

I sucked in my breath. 'What? WHAT? Entering the dance contest was my idea. You can't steal my idea, Scarlett. Who do you think you are?'

'I'm not stealing your idea,' said Scarlett. 'Any girl in the school can apply for the dance contest, as long as they have a squad. And Sophie and Primrose have agreed to make a squad with me. We already have a name. The Dream Team. You don't own dancing, Lottie. And you don't own these girls either.'

Farrah sniggered.

I felt sick. Totally sick.

'Primrose, Sophie,' I said. 'Can I talk to you for a minute? In private?'

Primrose and Sophie followed me outside.

'Listen, girls,' I said. 'Scarlett is being a bully. You have to stand up to her.'

'No she isn't, Lottie,' said Primrose. 'We're just trying to make things fair.'

'Fine,' I said. 'If that's how you're going to be. Do your baby routines with Scarlett. Miss Miel always picks my squad anyway. Because I'm head girl. So maybe I'll just find some other dancers.'

I walked off then, because I didn't want to cry in front of them.

When I got home from school that day, I went up to my bedroom and burst into tears.

Mum knocked on the door. 'Lottie. Can I come in?'

'NO!' I screamed.

Mum came in anyway and sat on my bed. 'What's wrong, love?'

'Lots of things,' I sniffed. 'Scarlett and Farrah are teasing me about my glasses. They keep whispering and laughing behind my back. And Scarlett has turned all my friends against me. I hate her so much. Farrah isn't even calling for me on the way to school.'

I burst into tears again.

'So why don't you call for Farrah tomorrow?' said Mum. 'Make a truce. I think it would be a good start.'

'But I never call for Farrah,' I said. 'She always calls for me.'

'Just give it a go,' said Mum. 'I'll give Kelly a ring and tell her to expect you tomorrow morning. Okay?' She gave me a kiss on my forehead. 'It'll all be just fine. You'll see.'

The next day, I called for Farrah.

She'd already left. Of course.

'I'm so sorry.' Kelly looked awkward. 'Farrah called for Scarlett and ... well, I know you and Scarlett have some issues. Maybe Farrah was trying to avoid an argument.'

It was so humiliating.

I jogged to school after that, just to make sure I got to Primrose and Sophie's houses first. I took the backroads to avoid Farrah and Scarlett, but then I saw them at the crossroads and had to duck into an alleyway.

Primrose and Sophie were awkward when I called for them. Like they were scared to talk or something. I suppose it was a bit difficult because we usually talk about dancing. But of course, now it's all weird.

I tried to tell Primrose and Sophie about how difficult Scarlett is making my life.

'We don't want to get involved,' said Sophie. 'We like dancing with both of you.'

Ugh.

When are those two going to wake up?

SCARLETT

Farrah and I walked to school together again this morning. It feels like a regular thing now. We called for Primrose and Sophie on the way, but they'd left already. Probably with Lottie, but we didn't talk about that. Instead, we shared ideas about my birthday party.

'The swimming pool will be all fixed up,' I said. 'So we can have pool games and pool-side fruit slushies. And a hot dog barbecue.'

'Wow, that's epic,' said Farrah.

'I know,' I said. 'And I haven't even told you the best part. Dad is flying over for the party.'

'Your dad is flying all the way over from America just for your birthday?' Farrah asked. 'He must be really cool.'

'He is.' I nodded. 'But it's the least he can do. Dad has missed so many of my birthday parties.'

'Does he send you presents, though?' asked Farrah.

'Not always,' I said. 'Or sometimes he'll send some weird present a week late, like rollerblades in the wrong size or a sock puppet set.'

'Let's get back to party planning.' Farrah clapped her hands together. 'Have you worked out a dress code yet?'

'I'm not really into dress codes,' I said. 'I'm more of a free spirit. Anyway, it's too late to add a dress code now. The invitations are printed. I have them in my bag.'

'You printed the invitations already?' said Farrah. 'Wow. That's fast work.'

'Jamie did it for me last night,' I said. 'He's on best behaviour at the moment.'

'So how about this?' said Farrah. 'When you hand out your invites, tell people about the dress code.'

'But there *isn't* a dress code,' I said.

'You *have* to do a dress code,' said Farrah. 'It's not a party without one. Hey, how about bikinis only?'

'Do bikinis count as a dress code?' I asked. 'I mean, doesn't every girl wear a bikini to go swimming?'

'Not at St Valentine's,' said Farrah. 'Most girls wear those sporty black one-piece costumes. You know, the kind you exercise in. It'll be really fun to wear *grown-up* swimwear for a change.' She lowered her voice. 'Lottie isn't allowed to wear *anything* that shows her midriff. Like, *ever*.'

We looked at each other and laughed.

'Lottie's clothes are so boring,' said Farrah. 'That's why you're so cool to hang out with, Scarlett. You have a totally grown-up wardrobe.'

When we got to school, Farrah suggested I hand out my birthday invitations right away.

Of course, Lottie glared at me as I handed out the invites. But what could I do? I didn't plan a birthday party to upset Lottie. It was bad timing that Lottie and Farrah had fallen out, but Lottie said it herself – we're old enough to have different friends without crying about it.

Lottie just needs to SUMO. Shut up and move on.

LOTTIE

Oh my god, what is WRONG with Scarlett?

This morning, she invited all *my* friends to her birthday party. She did it right in front of me too, smirking the whole time.

I waited for Scarlett to give me an invite. That would have been something at least. But she didn't.

It was so humiliating, listening to everyone gush about Scarlett's stupid pool party.

I wanted to burst into tears, but I held it in until I got home.

After school, Mum found me crying in my bedroom. Again.

'Scarlett is having a party,' I sobbed. 'She's invited all my friends, but not me.'

'That's appalling,' said Mum. 'What's wrong with this girl? First, she tells tales. Now, this. *And* you invited her to *your* party. I'm not standing for it. I'm going to this girl's house right now to talk to her mother.'

'I don't know if that's a good idea,' I sniffed.

'I do,' said Mum. 'If Scarlett's mother can't teach her good manners ... well, maybe it's up to me.'

Mum put on her fawn-coloured coat and went out. Half an hour later, she came home.

'You're going to Scarlett's party,' Mum told me. 'It's next Saturday. Scarlett's mother wasn't home, so I spoke to Scarlett instead. The two of us came to an understanding.'

'So ... Scarlett invited me to her party?' I asked.

'Yes,' said Mum. 'We had a little talk, and I helped Scarlett understand the pain and distress she was causing. We both agreed that an invitation was the best way forward.' Mum hesitated. 'Scarlett's big sister tried to interfere, but I think we came to an understanding there too.'

Oh. My. God.

Oh my god, oh my god, oh my god.

I didn't know whether to laugh or cry.

I liked the idea of Scarlett getting told off. But Mum

forcing her to invite me to her party ... oh no.

Later in the evening, Mum phoned Farrah's Mum. She talked about Scarlett using 'bullying' behaviour and girls forming 'cliques' and 'ganging up'.

'Lottie feels very unhappy,' Mum said. 'It would really help if Farrah included her in future. You know how girls can be at this age.'

Cassandra and I both rolled our eyes when Mum said that, but it worked. Farrah phoned five minutes later and gave me a stilted apology.

'I didn't know you were upset,' Farrah told me. 'You always put on that tough front. I'll see you tomorrow, okay? Mum told me to call for you.'

I didn't like the way Farrah said 'Mum told me to'. But I'm keeping my fingers crossed that everything will go back to normal now.

SCARLETT

Lottie's mother is totally crazy. She just came over and forced me to invite Lottie to *my* birthday party. And Mrs Collins said stuff about cliques and 'nasty' behaviour. Kind of making out I was picking on Lottie when it is totally the other way around.

Mrs Collins didn't shout or anything like that, but it was still obvious she thought I was this mean, rich girl picking on her daughter. It was so bad.

'Lottie says you're inviting all her friends to your party, but leaving her out,' said Mrs Collins. 'That's not a very kind thing to do, is it?'

'They're my friends too,' I squeaked.

'But these girls have been important to Lottie for longer,' said Mrs Collins. 'And now Lottie's hearing all these

Chinese whispers about a fabulous pool party and feeling very upset and left out.'

I don't think you're allowed to say Chinese whispers anymore because it's racist. But I was too scared to say anything.

'Look, I know you've had your hair done and you're wearing fabulous clothes and turning heads,' said Mrs Collins. 'But it's important not to get too full of yourself. Lottie invited you to her party, didn't she? The polite thing to do is to return the favour.'

There were so many things I wanted to say to that. Like, Mrs Singh *made* Lottie invite me. And Lottie didn't even write my name on the invite. And I am NOT full of myself. But the words sort of wouldn't come out.

'So will you invite Lottie to your party?' asked Mrs Collins. 'And then we can all be friends again?'

I could hardly say no. I mean, there was a full-grown adult on my doorstep, telling me what to do.

Mrs Collins shook my hand then, and said, 'I hope we can stop the nonsense now.'

When she left, Zara came running downstairs.

'Who was that?' she asked.

'The mum of a girl from school,' I said. 'She just made me invite her daughter to my birthday party.'

'You said no, right?' Zara eyeballed me.

I shook my head, tears running down my cheeks.

'Are you okay?' Zara asked.

'Not really,' I croaked. 'I don't want to invite this girl to my party. Dad is flying over. I want everything to be perfect.'

'Wait there.' Zara went running out after Lottie's mother.

A few minutes later, Zara came back looking annoyed.

'How can parents be so blind?' she said. 'Does that woman seriously think she's helping her daughter by forcing you to invite her to your party?'

'I know,' I said. 'It's so stupid. Lottie has fallen out with everyone, but her mother thinks it's everyone else's fault.'

'Make sure you give that girl hell at school,' said Zara. 'You have to take a stand, or everyone will walk all over you.' She hesitated. 'Is your dad definitely flying over for your party?'

'Yes,' I said.

Zara gave me a look.

'Dad really is coming,' I insisted. 'He's bought the airline tickets and everything.'

'I hope he makes it this time,' said Zara. 'Listen, Scarlett. I'm really sorry about your dad. You got a lousy deal.'

'Um ... okay.' I didn't really know what to say. I mean, Zara's dad isn't great either.

'It's not your fault,' said Zara, giving me serious eyes. 'You deserve better. And a better mother too.'

'Well, I'm fixing that,' I said. 'I'm going to win the Dolores Rush Dance Contest and come live near you in London. I have a dance squad now. Things are looking up.'

Zara gave me a kind smile. 'Isn't that a bit of a dream?'

'Maybe,' I said. 'But if you don't have a dream, how you gonna have a dream come true?'

Later that evening, Farrah called.

'I heard Lottie's mum came round your house tonight,' she said. 'What happened?'

'It was really bad,' I said. 'Mrs Collins made me invite Lottie to my party,'

'No way,' said Farrah. 'Well, get this. I have to walk to school with Lottie tomorrow. Mum's making me.'

'That's so unfair,' I said. 'I'll have no one to walk with.

And I have to invite Lottie to my party.'

'Why don't you call for Primrose and Sophie?' Farrah suggested. 'I'll make sure Lottie and I don't call for them.'

'Would they walk with me, though?' I asked. 'Aren't they more Lottie's friends?'

'No, they love you,' said Farrah. 'They think you're an awesome dancer, and between you and me, they prefer the Dream Team to the A-Squad. You're a lot more chilled. Hey – what are you going to say when you see Lottie at school tomorrow?'

'I'm going to give her hell,' I said, remembering Zara's words.

Farrah giggled.

'I mean it,' I said. 'I can't let Lottie get away with sending her mother to my house. When I see her at school, I'm going to tell her exactly what I think of her.'

The next day, I called for Primrose and Sophie on the way to school.

'Farrah says you're going to tell Lottie off today,' said Primrose, as we walked up the country track. 'Is that true?'

'Yes,' I said. 'Someone needs to stand up to Lottie. Don't you think?'

Neither of the girls said anything.

After a while, Primrose said, 'Listen, Scarlett. We know Lottie doesn't like you. But we just want you to know, we never join in with the things she says. We're stuck in the middle.'

'Lottie says things about me?' I asked. 'What things?'

'Like ... you're a bully and stuff,' said Primrose.

'Lottie told you guys I was a bully?' I demanded.

Primrose and Sophie fell silent. Then Primrose said,

'Well, yeah.'

I felt really angry. 'I'm a bully? Lottie sent her mother to my house last night. *That's* bullying.'

I'd already planned to confront Lottie at school, but now I had a lot more to say.

When we got to class, I waited by Lottie's seat with Primrose and Sophie. Then Farrah came running into class.

'Lottie's coming!' Farrah shouted. 'She's right outside.'

I felt anger welling up inside me.

When Lottie came into class, I marched right up to her.

'*You're* the bully,' I yelled. 'And everyone hates you.'

Then I took Lottie's seat at the front of the class, just to make the point, you know? *I'm* not scared of you.

You should have seen the look on Lottie's face when Farrah sat down next to me. She was *furious*. Lottie had to sit in the nerd chair next to Mrs Singh, which served her right.

For the rest of the day, everyone avoided Lottie. I felt a little bit sorry for her, but really, she was getting what she deserved.

LOTTIE

I felt totally ganged up on at registration today. Scarlett marched up to me and accused me of bullying her.

'You told your mother to come around my house last night,' she said.

'No,' I said, as forcefully as I could. 'I didn't *tell* Mum to do that. That is such a lie.'

'Are you calling Scarlett a liar?' said Farrah.

I couldn't believe Farrah said that. We'd just walked to school together, and everything seemed sort of alright. So why was she standing up for Scarlett all of a sudden?

I felt really panicked. 'Okay,' I said. 'Mum did go round to Scarlett's house. But I never asked her to. And she wasn't horrible or anything –'

'And you've been calling me a bully,' said Scarlett.

'I never said that.' I felt so flustered.

'You did,' said Scarlett. 'Primrose told me.'

I stared at Primrose, feeling sick.

'Stop glaring at us with your laser-ray glasses,' said Farrah. 'What are you trying to do, bore holes in us or something?'

Primrose did her weird, donkey laugh.

'Come on Farrah,' said Scarlett. 'Let's sit down.' Then she sat in my seat. It was a challenge, you know? Like, I'm taking your place, what are you going to do about it?

Just as I was about to tell Scarlett to get out of my seat, Farrah sat down next to her. Primrose and Sophie dropped down into their usual seats behind.

My stomach felt full of ice.

Mrs Singh came into the classroom then, register under her arm.

'Lottie,' she said. 'Why aren't you sitting down?'

'Scarlett took my seat,' I said.

'We don't have assigned seats in this class,' said Mrs Singh. 'It's free-flowing. You know that. First come, first served. It encourages you to get to school on time. Now sit down, please.'

I looked around the class.

Scarlett and Farrah were whispering and laughing at me. Primrose and Sophie wouldn't meet my eye. I couldn't sit at the back with Amina and Marianne, because ... well, I guess I haven't been all that friendly to Marianne in the past.

The only spare seat was the loner seat at the front, next to Mrs Singh.

I sat down, feeling scared and alone.

I couldn't wait for the school day to end, and it wasn't even nine o'clock.

A bad day turned into a bad week. Actually, the worst week of my life.

I had no one to walk to school with, no one to sit with and no one to hang out with at break and lunch. My so-called friends treated me like I had a disease.

At registration, everyone talked about Scarlett's stupid party, as if it were the social event of the year.

On Friday morning, the girls started gabbing away about bikinis.

'My bikini arrived last night,' said Farrah, glancing in my direction. 'Nike pink leopard print. Lucky it came on time, or I'd be *breaking* the dress code. Right, Scarlett? No one-piece swimming costumes allowed.'

Dress code? What dress code?

'We'll look so grown up,' Farrah continued, in a big, loud voice. 'Well, most of us will. Hey, what do you think Lottie will wear? I bet she'll come in a Peppa Pig swimming costume.'

All the girls laughed.

That did it. I was going to that party in a bikini if it killed me. I would show my friends that I'm not a baby and win them all back in time for the dance contest.

When I got home from school, I begged Mum to take me bikini shopping.

'Please, Mum,' I said. 'You don't understand how important

this is. All the girls will be wearing bikinis and Scarlett has turned everyone against me. I don't want to be the odd one out. I feel bad enough being the only girl wearing glasses. *Please.*'

'You know how your father feels about revealing clothes,' said Mum.

'Oh my *god*, Mum,' I shouted. 'You wear bikinis.'

'I'm a married woman,' said Mum. 'It's different. We don't want you sending out the wrong messages.'

I had a tantrum then. A mega tantrum. I screamed and shouted and threw things. I even smashed my bedside lamp – the one Aunt Jo gave me as a birthday present.

Dad came storming upstairs and roared at me for 'abominable behaviour'.

I ended up crying in my room again, which seems to be me every night at the moment.

Of course, Cassandra heard me crying and knocked on my door.

'What's going on?' she asked.

'I'm scared,' I said. 'I don't want to go to the party tomorrow.'

'Was it really bad today?' Cassandra asked.

'Awful,' I said.

'Everything happens for a reason, right?' said Cassandra. 'Maybe you're supposed to learn from this.'

'Learn what?' I asked. 'Learn how bad it feels to be picked on and left out?'

'Yes,' said Cassandra. 'I think that's exactly what you're supposed to learn. So you can understand what it's like to be on the other side of things. Maybe it will help you be a kinder person.'

'I am a kind person,' I said.

'You can be,' said Cassandra. 'But you can be really thoughtless too. Remember when Farrah moved to

Hiverstock? She started calling for you in the mornings, and you called her your stalker.'

'Oh yeah,' I said. 'I remember that. Farrah followed me everywhere when she moved here. Then we became friends.'

'Listen, Lottie,' said Cassandra. 'You don't know what it's like to be the new girl. Or the different girl. Or not as good at things. You've always been on the inside. And sometimes, you can come across as unfriendly.'

'I'm not unfriendly,' I said. 'I invited Scarlett to my party.'

'Oh yes,' said Cassandra. 'Because you were forced to. You didn't even buy Scarlett a cowboy hat. Listen, Lottie. I know you feel threatened by Scarlett. She's all shiny and new and exciting. And she lives in that big house. But that's no reason to be unkind.'

'I wasn't unkind.'

'Maybe you weren't outright mean,' Cassandra reasoned. 'But you weren't kind either.'

'None of this is helping me,' I said. 'All I want to do is win my friends back. And I will. Tomorrow at Scarlett's party. I just need a bikini.'

Cassandra shook her head. 'I already told you. Real friends can't be won or lost. Find some girls who care about you for you, not what you can do for them.'

But I don't want *other* friends.

I want *my* friends back.

SCARLETT

I don't usually get up early at weekends, but birthdays are different. I always set an alarm at 6am so I can make the most of the day.

Of course, I don't necessarily get up at 6am. This morning, I lay in bed for over an hour, imagining Dad's plane landing in London. Then I headed out to the garden to admire the swimming pool.

Our dingy, mouldy hole in the ground has become a gleaming, blue lagoon, and it couldn't be more perfect. Farrah and the girls will be coming over this morning to help me decorate, and I'm so excited to show them all the cool, crazy things Jamie and I bought for the garden.

At 7am, I called Dad's phone. I knew he should have landed by now and be making his way to our house.

'Hey, honey.' Dad picked up on the third ring and sounded sleepy.

'I can't wait to see you!' I squealed. 'Are you in a cab?'

'Oh honey,' Dad croaked. 'I'm not going to make it. There were some issues with my passport so I changed the flight. I'll come see you at Christmas. Okay?'

I swallowed, holding back the tears. 'Why didn't you tell me sooner?'

'I thought you'd be busy with your party and forget all about me,' said Dad. 'But hey – I sent you a really cool gift. The very latest iPhone. I even put DJ software on there. I know how much you love music.'

'Great,' I said. 'So you're missing my birthday and sending my present weeks late. Again.'

'Actually, I sent the phone last Saturday,' said Dad. 'Your mother has it. Listen, I gotta go. Love you so much.'

I cried when Dad hung up, then I pulled myself together and went into Mum's bedroom.

Mum sat up in bed like she'd had an electric shock. 'Scarlett? What are you doing up so early?'

Jamie pulled the duvet over his head and complained about being woken up.

'It's my birthday,' I said. 'Remember?'

'Of course.' Mum gave a tired nod. 'Your birthday. I know it's your birthday, Scarlett. I've just spent hundreds of pounds having the pool redone for you.'

'Dad said he sent me a present last week,' I said. 'Do you have it?'

'Oh yes.' Mum rubbed her dark eyelashes. 'He did send something. I put it in the wardrobe for you.'

Mum hunted around and found a brown box with my name on it. Inside was the very latest iPhone and some American candy. I knew Dad had touched the phone, which felt sort of special. But I still wished Dad could have visited in person.

'I'm assuming your father isn't coming?' said Mum.

'No,' I said. 'There was a problem with his passport.'

'There's always a problem with that guy,' said Jamie, from under the bedclothes. 'He never keeps his word.'

I felt angry then.

'At least Dad didn't walk out without saying goodbye, Jamie,' I said.

Mum made a weird noise, like a boiling kettle. 'Do you want this party today, Scarlett?' she hissed.

I swallowed my anger.

'I'm sorry, mother. I apologise for my outburst.' I walked out.

Zara was waiting for me at the top of the staircase.

'Well done,' she said.

'For what?' I asked.

'For standing up to Mum'

'I didn't stand up to Mum,' I said. 'I gave in. Like I always do.'

'But you said that thing about Jamie,' said Zara. 'I heard

you. You penetrated the web of lies. Come on. I'll make you a birthday breakfast.'

While we were having breakfast, Farrah called on my new phone.

'Happy birthday!' Farrah shouted. Then she sang the happy birthday song in a really loud voice. 'Are you looking forward to your party?'

'Not so much,' I said. 'Dad isn't coming.'

'No way,' said Farrah. 'Sorry. I know you were really excited to see him.'

'It's okay,' I said. 'I should be used to it by now. Dad never comes. I'm trying to focus on the positive. There will be lots of cool people at my party.'

Farrah snorted. 'Yes. And Lottie.'

We both laughed.

'Are you worried Lottie might ruin your birthday?' Farrah asked.

'No way,' I said. 'I don't get why everyone is so afraid of Lottie. She's just this short girl with a pointy face and a bossy voice.'

'And angry librarian glasses,' said Farrah.

We laughed again.

'What do you think Lottie will wear to the party?' Farrah asked. 'There's no way her parents will buy her a bikini.'

'Lottie's so competitive,' I said. 'I bet she cuts her swimming costume in half to make a bikini.'

'Yes!' said Farrah. 'That's exactly the sort of thing she'd do.'

We laughed about that for a long time.

PART 3

FIGHT TO THE DEATH

When a young queen bee is born, she seeks out rival queens and kills them.

LOTTIE

ON THE MORNING of Scarlett's party, I woke up feeling nervous.

I didn't want to see Scarlett or my friends, and I definitely didn't want to be the only girl at the party in a one-piece swimming costume.

I imagined Scarlett and Farrah, whispering about me and calling me a baby.

Ugh. It was just horrible.

For a crazy moment, I thought about cutting my black, Slazenger swimming costume in half with Mum's sewing scissors. After all, a bikini is just a cut-up swimming costume, right? Then I realised the bottom half wouldn't have elastic and would fall down. Not a good look.

At breakfast, I was red-eyed and unhappy, chewing my cereal like a sad cow.

'Don't look so glum, Lottie,' said Mum.

'What's there to be happy about?' I asked. 'I'm going to look like a total idiot today.'

Mum smiled. 'Well actually, I have a little surprise for you. Don't tell your father. But I went shopping.'

'No way, Mum,' said Cassandra. 'No more secrets from Dad. This is so unhealthy. You know what will happen. Dad will find out and you'll end up having a horrible argument.'

'Your father won't find out,' said Mum. 'Lottie is having a hard time. I'm trying to support her.'

Mum went upstairs and returned with a black bikini. 'Ta-da!'

'No way.' I grinned from ear to ear. 'You got me a bikini? Mum, you are such a star.'

The bikini was very sporty looking, with a tiny white

jaguar near the shoulder. The top half was quite long, but that was okay. It was still a two-piece.

'Thank you so much.' I threw my arms around Mum. 'You are the best mother in the whole wide world.'

'Mum,' said Cassandra. 'I don't think this is good parenting.'

I had a feeling Cassandra might be right, but I wasn't complaining.

'This is great,' I said. 'I'll go to the party and get all my friends back. And then we'll win the dance contest and live happily ever after.'

'Of course you will,' said Mum. 'I never doubted it.'

That afternoon, Mum walked me to Scarlett's house. I wore my new bikini under my clothes and carried Scarlett's gift – a hardback copy of Little Women. I hate giving books as presents, but Mum thinks they're a 'sophisticated gift'.

I felt nervous walking up to Scarlett's house. It's so much bigger and fancier than ours, and I could already hear girls chattering and laughing in the garden.

There was a note on the front door:

'Please go through the side gate.'

The note was decorated with fireworks and a glitter rainbow.

'I'll leave you here,' said Mum.

'Please come round the back with me,' I begged.

'My goodness, this isn't like you at all,' said Mum. 'You're usually so confident.'

As Mum and I walked down the side of the house, I started to feel really nervous. I felt even worse when I saw lots of girls were in the garden already, eating food, sitting on sun loungers and splashing around in the pool. I got the feeling everyone had been there for a while.

Farrah, Primrose and Sophie were by the buffet table, chattering away and loading their plates with sushi. I waved, and they all gave me awkward waves back. Then Farrah turned to Primrose and they both giggled.

My stomach dropped.

'See what I mean?' I told Mum.

'What are you talking about?' said Mum. 'Your friends just waved at you. It's Scarlett who's being rude. She should have come over and welcomed you to the party by now.'

Scarlett was walking around in a gold bikini, handing out drinks. Like she was a celebrity or something. She looked absolutely great. Her red hair hung in soft, shining curls and her tanned, athletic body looked good in gold.

Mum gave me a hug and told me I'd be fine.

'Just smile and be yourself,' said Mum. 'Why don't you talk to Farrah? FARRAH!'

Mum started waving then. It was so embarrassing.

Farrah turned around, a plate of sushi in her hand. She gave Mum an awkward wave, then shook her head like, *what is she on*?

'How's Kelly doing?' Mum called out.

Farrah put on a fake smile. 'Oh, fine. Thanks, Mrs Collins.'

'I haven't seen her in a while,' said Mum. 'Tell her we must meet up.'

Farrah nodded.

'See?' said Mum. 'Farrah's being okay. I bet you'll be getting on just fine by the end of the party. I'll see you soon.'

When Mum left, Scarlett noticed me, but she didn't come over and say hello.

I took a deep breath and tried not to feel angry. Instead, I walked around the garden, acting confident. I have to say, Scarlett had made everything look fantastic. There were hanging lights and fake palm trees and inflatable flamingos. It was really fun.

I don't like raw fish, so I got some weird star-shaped crackers from the buffet and just sort of stood around, feeling scared and self-conscious.

Then Scarlett clapped her hands together. 'Hey everyone! Time for pool games.'

I changed out of my dress, took my glasses off and headed towards the pool.

'Nice bikini, Lottie,' said Farrah. 'Is it actually a bikini? Or is it a swimming costume cut in half?'

Scarlett started laughing. Really laughing. Soon, she was actually crying with laughter. Holding her stomach, tears rolling down her cheeks. Some of the other girls joined in, even though they didn't know what was funny.

I totally froze. Oh my god. How did Scarlett know about my cut-up swimming costume idea? Could she read my mind or something?

I went bright red.

'Wait.' Scarlett wiped her eyes. 'Before we get in the water, I want to take a picture of everyone with my new phone.'

'Hang on a minute,' said Farrah. 'Lottie can't be in the picture. She's not following the dress code.'

'I am,' I said, in an indignant voice. 'I'm wearing a bikini.'

'That is so not a bikini,' said Farrah. 'The top half is so *long*.'

'So?' I said. 'It's still a two-piece.'

'Okay. Prove it.' Farrah came behind me. Before I knew what was happening, Farrah was pulling up my bikini top. I don't think Farrah meant to pull it all the way up, but as I twisted out of the way, I ended up showing my whole top half.

I screamed. Before I could put my bikini back in place, Scarlett had taken the group shot.

Oh my GOD.

'Delete that picture,' I screeched, pulling down my bikini top. 'Right *now*.'

'No way!' Scarlett laughed at her phone. 'Lottie. You just totally flashed the camera.'

'DELETE THAT PICTURE!' I shouted.

'Delete it, Scarlett,' said Amina.

'Scarlett doesn't have to delete anything,' said Farrah. 'It's *her* phone. And this is her house. She owns the copyright.'

Panic beat in my chest.

Scarlett turned her back on me and started tapping things into her phone. 'I'll just share this picture with the WhatsApp party group.'

'Hey,' said Farrah. 'Lottie's not in the WhatsApp group. She doesn't have her own phone. So we'd better invite her *dad*.'

'Don't you dare.' I marched up to Scarlett and snatched her phone.

'Give that to me!' Scarlett tried to grab her phone back.

Before I could think about it, I threw Scarlett's phone onto the tiled ground. The phone bounced a few times, then landed face up, a spiderweb of broken glass on the screen.

The world froze.

'My phone!' screamed Scarlett. 'My dad got me that

phone. What is wrong with you? Do you know what, Lottie? EVERYONE thinks you're bossy and a total baby. They all hate you.'

That's when I really lost it. I pounced on Scarlett, tearing at her hair, scratching her face. Honestly, I wanted to hurt her so badly. I'd just had enough.

I remember Scarlett screaming, and then this older girl with black hair pulling me off.

I must have looked a total mess because I had scratches and bruises from the patio and tears running down my face.

Amina wrapped me in a towel.

'Come on, Lottie,' she said. 'I'll walk you home. You need a nice, hot cup of tea.'

My clothes, shoes and glasses are still at Scarlett's house, but they're the least of my worries right now.

How on earth am I going to face everyone on Monday morning?

SCARLETT

Lottie Collins is a monster.

A total monster.

I knew she could be mean, but I had no idea she was actually dangerous.

Lottie could have killed me. I mean, seriously. We were right by the swimming pool. I could have fallen in, cracked my head open and drowned. If Zara hadn't pulled Lottie off me, I don't know what would have happened.

I now have a bald spot the size of a penny right near my ear, because Lottie yanked a huge lump of my hair out. My top lip is swollen and I have scratch marks all over my neck.

It was a totally vicious attack.

Thank goodness Amina was there to walk Lottie home. No one else wanted to go anywhere near that psycho.

When Lottie left, Zara told the girls to sit with me while she called the NHS emergency number.

'Watch out for signs of concussion,' said Zara. 'Dizziness, sleepiness, headaches ... If she throws up, come and get me straight away.'

The girls gathered around, telling me how awful it all was.

'I can't believe Lottie did this on your *birthday*,' said Sophie. 'It was so vicious. My heart is racing.'

'Lottie's parents will have to buy you a new phone,' said Farrah. 'Lottie's dad will be furious.'

'No one can replace that phone,' I said. 'Dad sent it from New York. He packed it up himself. With his own hands.'

I started crying then. Really crying and shaking. I think it was the shock, you know?

The girls tried to make me feel better.

'Lottie will get what's coming to her,' said Farrah. 'Her dad is really strict.'

'The bald spot doesn't show at all, Scarlett,' said Sophie. 'Honestly.'

'Hey, *look*.' Farrah went over to the poolside. 'Lottie left her clothes and shoes behind. And her *glasses*.' She picked up all Lottie's things and threw them in the swimming pool.

I gave a shocked laugh as sandals, dress and glasses slowly sunk to the bottom.

'Good riddance,' said Farrah.

Then Amina came back and told us off for throwing Lottie's things in the swimming pool.

'I know Lottie did wrong,' said Amina. 'But she was provoked. You should never have pulled up Lottie's bikini,

Farrah. That's assault. And taking a naked photograph of a minor is against the law.'

'Oh my god, Amina,' said Farrah. 'We were just *joking* with Lottie. She needs to get a sense of humour.'

I felt really annoyed with Amina. I mean, there I was, shaking and covered in scratches and bruises, and Amina was practically saying it was my fault.

'Lottie is very sorry for what happened,' said Amina. 'She was crying on the way home.'

'It's too late for sorry,' said Farrah. 'Lottie scarred Scarlett for life. And broke her new phone.'

I started crying again, and everyone cooed and clucked around me and told me I was brave.

Amina left then, and I didn't miss her at all. I can see why Farrah finds her so annoying.

For the rest of the party, we talked about Lottie. The girls dredged up memories from years and years ago. Little things Lottie had said or done when they were younger.

'Lottie hit me on the head with a *wooden* toy at nursery,' Primrose told us. 'She's always been vicious.'

Even Marianne joined in.

'The A-Squad is so over,' said Farrah. 'It's Dream Team all the way from now on.' She turned to Primrose and Sophie. 'Are you two going to dance with a vicious psychopath? Or are you going to commit to the winning team?'

'Commit to the winning team,' said Primrose.

Sophie nodded.

'Okay,' said Farrah. 'It's settled then. Lottie has no one to dance with, so the Dream Team will go through to the dance contest. It has to. Happy birthday, Scarlett. You got your wish.'

'You're kidding,' I said. 'Really? I'll be in the contest? For certain?'

'Unless Lottie gets another squad together,' said Primrose.

'But I don't think she will,' said Sophie. 'Lottie needs everything to be perfect. And the contest is only ...' She counted on her fingers. 'Two weeks away. She's not going to train anyone new in that time. Her standards are too high.'

'I can't believe this,' I said. 'We're entering the contest together? Oh my god. What if we *win*? I can live in London!'

'I think we stand a chance,' said Sophie. 'A good chance.'

It's weird how life goes sometimes.

From a truly horrible birthday party came the best present I could have wished for.

LOTTIE

After the party, I couldn't stop crying. I cried for hours in my bedroom, while Mum and Dad talked about me downstairs. Of course, there was a huge argument about the bikini, and Dad called Mum all sorts of horrible names. Then Mum and Dad took turns coming upstairs to tell me about my bad behaviour.

I have to pay for Scarlett's phone out of my savings and I'm not allowed to go to the pizza park for a month. Which doesn't really matter, because I have no friends to go with anyway.

'Why did you do it?' Mum kept asking me. 'Why?'

Of course, I didn't mention the naked photograph or Scarlett's threats about WhatsApp. I would have died of embarrassment.

After many hours of crying, Mum and Dad made me come downstairs.

'You need to get a hold of yourself,' said Dad. 'And tomorrow, you'll phone Scarlett and apologise for ruining her birthday.'

I cried even harder then. I knew I needed to apologise, but I felt like Scarlett should apologise too. If she hadn't taken that photograph, the fight would never have happened.

On Sunday morning, Mum called Scarlett's mother and explained that I would like to apologise to Scarlett. Then she put me on the phone.

I heard Scarlett's voice: 'What do *you* want?'

'I'm really sorry,' I said. 'I'm sorry about your iPhone too. I'll buy you a new one out of my own money.'

Mum snatched the phone then and apologised on behalf of the whole family. 'And Scarlett, please tell us the phone make and model so we can replace it.'

There was a long silence.

Then Mum said, 'Oh. Right. I didn't know that. I'm sure if Lottie had known what that phone meant to you ... anyway. Lottie is being severely punished for this. We're not taking it lightly. She won't be allowed to go to the pizza park for a month.'

There was another long silence. Then Mum looked at the phone. 'Oh. She's hung up.'

'What did she say?' I asked.

'She's angry,' said Mum. 'And she has every right to be. Lottie, is there something you're not telling me? I feel like there's more to this than meets the eye. To *attack* someone so viciously ... it's just not like you.'

I put my head in my hands. 'Just leave it, Mum. Okay? I've said sorry. What more do you want?'

'I think you're going to have a hard time at school on Monday,' said Mum. 'But hold your head up high. You've apologised. You're buying this girl a new phone. There's nothing else you can do.'

School.

The idea of it makes me feel sick.

I always thought of myself as a strong person. But maybe I was only strong because everyone around me let me feel strong. And now they're not on my side anymore ... I have no idea who I am.

SCARLETT

Monday came around super quick. Too quick, really. I needed more time to calm down.

I was so furious about my phone and my injuries, and I admit it – I wanted to hurt Lottie.

Badly.

When Farrah called for me in the morning, she suggested we get Lottie on the way to school.

'Lottie ruined your birthday party,' said Farrah. 'And she's given you scars for life. You're not going to let her get away with that, are you?'

'No,' I said.

'So teach her a lesson,' said Farrah.

The idea made me feel powerful. Like a superhero, righting wrongs.

When we called for Primrose and Sophie, they asked how I was feeling.

'Angry,' I said. 'I'm going to talk to Lottie before school.'

'Just talk?' said Farrah.

'Maybe,' I said. 'We'll see what happens.'

Primrose and Sophie didn't say 'great', but they didn't say 'bad idea' either.

'Let's wait for Lottie in the lane,' said Farrah. 'No one from school can see us there.'

When we got to the country track, we waited. And waited. Lots of other girls walked past and asked us what we were doing. We told them we were meeting someone.

After twenty minutes of waiting, I was sure Lottie wasn't coming.

'She must have wimped out and taken a sick day,' said Farrah. 'What a coward. She can give it out but she can't take it back.'

Just as we were about to leave for school, Farrah hissed, 'Look! There she is.'

A navy blob came up the path towards us.

'It's definitely Lottie,' said Primrose. 'I can see her nerd glasses.' She glanced at me for approval.

I laughed.

As Lottie came closer, Farrah shouted, 'HEY! Lottie. Scarlett has something to say to you.'

Lottie looked afraid. She tried to walk past us, but I stood in her way.

'Hey,' I said. 'Didn't you hear what Farrah said? I want to talk to you.'

'I already said sorry,' said Lottie. 'What more do you want?'

'Everyone at school thinks you're a total bully,' I said.

'I'm a bully?' said Lottie. 'What do you call this? Ganging up on me on the way to school.'

'Did you hear that?' said Farrah. 'Lottie thinks *we're* bullies.'

We all laughed.

'I told you I was sorry!' Lottie screeched.

'Sorry isn't good enough,' I said. 'If you EVER ruin anything from my dad again, you're going to get really hurt.'

'Go on then,' said Lottie, sticking out her stupid, pointy little chin. 'If you're so tough. Hit me and get it over with.'

I kind of didn't know what to do then. Luckily, Farrah helped me out. She stepped forward and pulled Lottie's hair.

Lottie made this stupid noise: 'Eeeerog!' She shoved Farrah's hand away.

'She hit me!' said Farrah. 'Did you see that?'

I stepped forward then, and Lottie ran. She tried to make it look like she was walking really fast, but it was definitely running.

We all laughed as Lottie raced up the path. It was like slaying a monster, you know?

Primrose kept doing impressions of the noise Lottie made: 'Eeeerog! Eeeeerog!'

It was so funny.

When we got to school, Farrah and I sat together as normal. Primrose and Sophie sat behind us.

Lottie had to sit alone again.

When Mrs Singh called my name in the register, she looked at my bruised, scratched face and said, 'My word, Scarlett. What happened to you?'

Farrah put her hand up. 'Can we talk to you about it after the register, Mrs Singh?'

'Yes, of course,' said Mrs Singh.

Lottie put her hand up. 'Can I talk to you too, Mrs Singh?'

'Let me talk to Scarlett and Farrah first,' said Mrs Singh. 'I can talk to you a little later. Okay, Lottie?'

Lottie looked away like she was going to cry.

After Mrs Singh called the register, she waved Farrah and me into her counsellor's office.

'How can I help you girls?' asked Mrs Singh, as we all sat on colourful, plastic chairs.

'Lottie attacked Scarlett, Mrs Singh,' said Farrah. 'I was there. It was awful.'

Mrs Singh's brown eyes swam with concern, but she didn't say anything. She just nodded for Farrah to continue.

'It happened at Scarlett's birthday party,' Farrah went on. '*And* Lottie broke Scarlett's phone. She just went totally insane.'

'I can't deal with things that happen outside of school,' said Mrs Singh. 'But I can listen, and maybe help you girls become friends again.'

Farrah snorted. 'That's not going to happen. And anyway, things *have* happened at school. Lottie threw me out of her dance squad. Just because I was walking to school with Scarlett. And on the way to school just now, Lottie tried to start a fight with Scarlett. Lottie said, go on, hit me. And when I tried to stick up for Scarlett, Lottie *shoved* me.'

Mrs Singh turned to me, then. 'You haven't said very much, Scarlett. Is there anything you want to talk about? Why would Lottie attack you? Especially at a birthday party, of all places?'

'Scarlett made a joke and Lottie took it the wrong way,' said Farrah.

Mrs Singh laughed. 'That's a very clever trick, Scarlett. You talked without moving your mouth at all.'

The bell rang then.

'What a shame,' said Mrs Singh, checking her watch. 'I was hoping we could bring Lottie in here and see what she has to say about all this. But maybe we can do that at break time –'

'No way,' said Farrah. 'Lottie will just twist everything.'

Mrs Singh sighed. 'Right. Well, I suppose you should get to your lessons. What do you have now?'

'Science,' I said.

Mrs Singh sighed. 'This is sad, girls. Especially with the dance contest coming up. Farrah, you and Lottie usually do such a wonderful job of representing our school –'

'I'm not dancing with Lottie anymore.' Farrah put an arm around my shoulder. 'I've switched to Scarlett's squad. The Dream Team.'

'So close to the contest?' said Mrs Singh. 'Is that wise?'

'What else can I do?' said Farrah. 'Lottie is impossible.'

Mrs Singh laughed. 'Once upon a time, mobile telephones and automatic doors were the stuff of science fiction. Nothing is impossible, girls. Now go to class, and I'll think about healthy ways to settle your differences.'

LOTTIE

Scarlett ambushed me on my way to school this morning. It was horrible. She threatened me, and Farrah pulled my hair, really hard. Hard enough to yank my head back.

I ended up running the rest of the way to school. Four against one is scary and also totally unfair. Maybe I deserve to get hit by Scarlett, but the other girls are nothing to do with it.

When I got to school, I felt so alone and shaken up.

Registration was awful. Obviously. Lots of whispering and giggling behind my back. Then Scarlett and Farrah asked to talk to Mrs Singh privately in her counsellor's office.

That felt awful because I knew full well they were talking about me.

When the bell rang, Scarlett and Farrah were still talking to Mrs Singh, so I had to go to science without telling Mrs Singh my side of things.

Scarlett and Farrah were late to science. When Mr Spinny asked them why, Farrah said, 'We had to see Mrs Singh. About a BULLY.' And looked right at me.

I spent the rest of science class feeling really worried. What had Scarlett and Farrah told Mrs Singh about me? Had they talked about the party? They must have done. Oh my god. Would Mrs Singh tell Miss Miel? Would I lose my head girl badge?

The moment science finished, I ran to Mrs Singh's classroom. I didn't even knock on the door. I just ran inside, out of breath and panicked.

Mrs Singh wasn't teaching a class, but she was about to take a bite from a chocolate chip muffin.

'Lottie?' Mrs Singh looked from me to the muffin. 'Can I help you?'

'What did Scarlett and Farrah say about me?' I asked.

Mrs Singh gave a little sigh and put her muffin down. 'You'd better come into my office, Lottie. I was going to send for you today, actually. So you've saved me a job.'

Mrs Singh's counsellor's office was full of stress toys, like Rubik's Cubes and squeezy blue things. There were beanbags in the corner and a board on the wall showing faces with different emotions.

Mrs Singh sat at a desk with a rainbow-striped tablecloth over it and gestured for me to sit opposite.

'So, tell me all about it,' said Mrs Singh. 'What's happening?'

I just stood there.

I wanted to defend myself. To tell Mrs Singh about the photograph and all the other horrible things that had happened over the last few weeks. But it was all so embarrassing and pathetic. Tears welled up. I fought so hard to hold them back, but I could feel them leaking down my cheeks.

Mrs Singh gave me an encouraging smile. 'Is there something you want to tell me?'

I couldn't speak. There was a huge lump in my throat. I'd meant to be calm and confident, and tell Mrs Singh how awful Scarlett and Farrah had been. But I knew the words would be teary and pathetic. And maybe I'd sound like I was lying or making a big deal of things.

'Do you want to tell me about what happened at Scarlett's birthday party?' Mrs Singh asked, in an encouraging voice.

I managed to splutter: 'Please don't tell Miss Miel I was fighting. She'll take my head girl badge.'

'We don't discipline things that happen outside of school,' said Mrs Singh. 'If I did, I'd never get any sleep, and I don't get enough as it is. Are you *sure* there's nothing you'd like to tell me?'

I shook my head. Why couldn't I hold it together?

'You put yourself under a lot of pressure, Lottie,' said Mrs Singh. 'Maybe this dance contest is too much, on top of everything else.'

That did it. I burst into tears.

'No one ... will dance with me anyway,' I sobbed. 'So ... I have to w-withdraw my application.'

I turned and ran out of the office before Mrs Singh could reply. I ran all the way home, my school bag bang, banging on my back.

I didn't care about missing Spanish or getting into

trouble. I didn't care about anything except hiding my stupid, pathetic crying face.

When I got home, Cassandra was sitting at the kitchen table, eating a cheese sandwich and reading a French novel.

'What are you doing here?' Cassandra asked.

'I'm sick.' I sat down at the kitchen table. 'What are *you* doing here? Shouldn't you be at college?'

'I have three free periods on Mondays,' said Cassandra. 'So I came home to study.' She gave me serious eyes. 'You don't look sick. You do know Mum will be home after lunch, don't you?'

I froze. 'I thought Mum worked all day on Mondays.'

'No, she changed it ages ago,' said Cassandra. 'Monday is her half-day now.'

'Please tell Mum I'm sick,' I said. 'You know she'll believe you.'

'Only if you tell me what's going on,' said Cassandra.

My lip began to wobble. 'I just ... couldn't stand being at school any longer. The girls there are so horrible.'

Cassandra put her book down. 'This is serious, Lottie. If you're missing school ... I mean, it's more than just an argument between friends.'

Tears came. 'The girls waited for me on the way to school today and Farrah pulled my hair.'

Cassandra gasped. 'Farrah did *what*?'

'But I deserved it,' I spluttered. 'I mean, I pulled Scarlett's hair right out.'

'That's for you and Scarlett to sort out,' said Cassandra. 'What's it got to do with Farrah?'

'Well, she was standing up for her friend.'

'Uh huh,' said Cassandra. 'How else has Farrah stood up for her friend?'

I hesitated. 'Promise you won't tell Mum and Dad?'

'Of course I won't,' said Cassandra. 'You know me better than that.'

I swallowed. 'At Scarlett's party, Farrah pulled my bikini up in front of everyone.'

'No *way*,' said Farrah.

I nodded. 'And then Scarlett took a photograph.'

'WHAT?'

'Don't make me say it again,' I hissed. 'It's so embarrassing. Scarlett said she was going to put the picture on WhatsApp.'

'Oh my god,' said Cassandra. 'No wonder you lost your temper.'

'I hate Scarlett so much,' I said. 'Everything was fine until she came along.'

'Was it?' said Cassandra. 'Because from what I can see, Farrah's always been mean. You just didn't notice because she was sucking up to you.'

'Farrah wasn't sucking up,' I said. 'She was my friend.'

'If she was your friend, she wouldn't have pulled your bikini up,' said Cassandra. 'Those girls are ganging up on you and it's bullying. It needs to be dealt with.'

I started crying even harder then. 'But I deserve all this, Cassandra. I was really mean to Scarlett. I organised my pink party on the same day she was having *her* party. On purpose. And I was unkind to Scarlett at my party. I really left her out.'

'Well, I guess now you know why the girls are being horrible to you,' said Cassandra.

'Thanks a lot, big sister,' I said. 'Just what I need right now.'

'I don't mean it like that,' said Cassandra. 'What I'm saying is ... well, we can all be horrible sometimes, right? I mean, why were you unkind to Scarlett?'

I sniffed. 'I was jealous. Because she was all shiny and new and it looked like she was stealing Farrah away.'

'Well done for admitting that,' said Cassandra. 'Listen, Lottie. You have to tell Mum and Dad what's going on. They can phone the school and get everything sorted out. This is too much for you to handle alone. Four against one isn't right.'

'I can't tell Mum and Dad about the bikini thing, Cassandra,' I said. 'Honestly. It's just so embarrassing.'

'Count this as an act of courage,' said Cassandra. 'Remember our family motto? Fortune favours the brave. Be brave and tell the truth.'

When Mum came home after lunch, I told her everything. The bikini incident, the photo, the walk to school ambush, the leaving out and teasing and name-calling. Everything.

Mum was shocked. She phoned Dad, who was angry. Then Mum called the school.

TALK TO THE AUTHOR

Excuse the interruption ...

HELLO THERE. I'm Suzy, the author of this book. Thank you so much for reading and I hope you're enjoying the story so far.

I love hearing from readers, so if you have questions about this book or anything at all, you can email:

contact@suzykquinn.com

You can also friend me on Facebook.com/suzykquinn

Come along and say hello,

Lots of love,

Suzy xx

SCARLETT

AT BREAK TIME, the gossip was all over the school – Lottie Collins had run home.

Everyone was shocked.

'Lottie never even has sick days,' said Sophie, as we headed to the dance studio. 'I can't believe she left the building *without permission*.'

'We must have really upset her,' I said.

'Oh, whatever,' said Farrah. 'Lottie is just being dramatic. She's trying to make us look bad. Don't fall for it. Let's just go practise our dancing.'

Towards the end of break time, Mrs Singh poked her head into the dance studio.

'Girls?' she said. 'Can I have a word?'

We all looked at each other.

Mrs Singh closed the dance studio door. 'Actually, it's nice and private in here, isn't it? Let's have a quick talk before you go to your next lesson.'

'What about?' asked Farrah.

'I'll get to that,' said Mrs Singh, taking a seat on the rubbery floor. 'Come and sit down, girls.'

We sat cross-legged by Mrs Singh.

'Now girls.' Mrs Singh gave us serious, brown eyes. 'Can anyone tell me what bullying is?'

'A bigger person pushing around a smaller person,' said Primrose. 'And stealing their lunch money. And calling them horrible names. And –'

'Do you know something, Primrose?' said Mrs Singh. 'That kind of bullying doesn't happen as much as you might think. The bullying I see is usually more subtle. For example, leaving people out. Has anyone ever left someone out? Because they felt angry with them?'

Farrah's hand shot into the air. 'Lottie leaves me out of things all the time. She threw me out of her dance squad just to be mean.'

Mrs Singh gave a kind nod. 'Yes, it feels very hurtful, doesn't it? I'd say that was a type of bullying. What about whispering and giggling. Do you think that's bullying?'

Farrah looked uncomfortable.

'And how about waiting for someone on the way to school?' said Mrs Singh. 'Do you think that might feel like bullying?'

More silence.

'What about hair pulling?' asked Mrs Singh.

Primrose and Sophie both nodded.

'And what about if others watched hair pulling and did nothing?' said Mrs Singh.

'I don't think so, Mrs Singh,' said Primrose. 'You can't be a bully if you haven't done anything.'

'Well, I'd have to disagree with you, Primrose,' said Mrs Singh. 'People who don't stop bad behaviour are just as bad as those who do bad things. We must do the right thing, even if it's frightening or uncomfortable.'

Beside me, all the girls looked awkward. Primrose was bright red and Sophie looked at her hands.

I felt bad too because I knew this was about Lottie. But *I* hadn't bullied Lottie. She'd bullied me. Mrs Singh had got it all wrong. Okay, yes. Farrah had pulled Lottie's hair. But she totally deserved it. I mean, Lottie pulled my hair *right* out.

'Listen, girls,' said Mrs Singh. 'Lottie Collins withdrew her dance contest entry this morning. Why might she have done that?'

'No way.' Farrah grabbed my arm. 'Scarlett, that means we're definitely through. Woo! Go Dream Team!'

I should have felt joy bubble up in my chest, but I felt guilty. For Lottie to withdraw from the contest after months of hard work … well, she must be really upset. I didn't feel good about that.

Mrs Singh gave Farrah cold, hard teacher's eyes. 'Not the reaction I was looking for, Farrah. And as a matter of fact, nobody is going through to the dance contest right now.'

Primrose gasped. '*No* one?'

'That's right,' said Mrs Singh. 'I've spoken to Miss Miel. The dance contest is supposed to help you girls learn co-operation and teamwork. If you're falling out over it, we feel the best thing to do is cancel our entry.'

'But that's not *fair*,' cried Farrah.

'So, tell me what would be fair,' said Mrs Singh.

'For us four to go forward,' said Farrah. 'The Dream Team.'

'But what about Lottie?' asked Mrs Singh. 'How will that make her feel?'

Farrah shrugged. 'That's her problem.'

'I'm sorry you think that way, Farrah,' said Mrs Singh. 'Okay, girls. Off to class.'

LOTTIE

The next day, I felt really nervous about going to school.

'You'll be fine,' Mum told me. 'Mrs Singh has already talked to some of the girls. They'll leave you alone from now on.'

I wasn't totally sure about that, but thankfully, no one was waiting for me on the country track.

During registration, no one was friendly, but no one whispered or giggled either.

I wondered if this was how bullying issues get solved. The girls would leave me alone, and I'd just be one of those weird kids with no friends. I didn't like that idea much, but it was better than being picked on.

After Mrs Singh took the register, she smiled at the class. 'We have five minutes before lessons,' she said. 'Talk amongst yourselves. Lottie. Scarlett. Can I borrow you, please?'

My heart started beating really fast.

'This won't take long.' Mrs Singh stood up and opened the door to her counselling office. 'Come on. I don't bite.' She gave me an encouraging smile.

Scarlett and I trotted into Mrs Singh's office.

'Right girls.' Mrs Singh sat on the edge of her rainbow-coloured desk. 'I'll get straight to the point. Does anyone want to tell me about a photograph?'

Scarlett looked awkward.

I blushed bright red. I'd really hoped things could be sorted out without having to mention *that* photograph.

'I hear an indecent photograph was taken of Lottie,' Mrs Singh continued. 'And shared on a WhatsApp group.'

'The WhatsApp thing never happened,' said Scarlett, quickly. 'Yes, okay. I said something about WhatsApp. But I was never going to do it.'

'Ah,' said Mrs Singh. 'So there was a photograph?'

Scarlett looked away. 'I was taking a group shot, and Lottie sort of ... I mean she flashed the camera.'

'I did not,' I said. 'Farrah pulled up my bikini.'

'Okay, okay,' said Scarlett. 'But I didn't know that was going to happen. It was just bad timing that I took the shot at that exact moment. I was never going to post that picture. I just said that thing about WhatsApp to annoy you.'

'Why didn't you and Farrah tell me about the photograph when you came to see me yesterday?' asked Mrs Singh.

Scarlett didn't say anything.

'And why didn't you tell me that Farrah indecently assaulted Lottie?' asked Mrs Singh.

'Indecent assault?' Scarlett's eyes widened. 'We didn't –'

'Yes,' said Mrs Singh. 'Farrah pulled up Lottie's bikini.'

'But Lottie attacked me,' I said. '*That's* assault.'

'It certainly is,' said Mrs Singh. 'But so is removing someone's clothing without permission. And taking a *photograph*. If that photograph was distributed ... well, you could have gone to prison.'

'Okay, I shouldn't have made the WhatsApp joke,' said Scarlett, in a scared voice. 'You're making it out to be this massive deal –'

'It *is* a massive deal,' said Mrs Singh. 'Look, I know we're more open-minded to gender these days, and I don't want to put people into boxes. But what if a group of *boys* did that to Lottie? What would you think then?'

I started crying then. Not noisy crying, but sniffing tears leaking out. It was so humiliating.

Scarlett's brown eyes turned sad. 'I'm so sorry. I didn't think about it like that. I never would have posted that photograph, Lottie. Honestly, I wouldn't.'

'Well, how was I supposed to know that?' I sniffed.

'Maybe if you'd got to know me better,' said Scarlett, 'you would understand that I'm a very kind person with a lot of feelings.'

'You don't seem kind to me,' I said. 'You turned all my friends against me. You've made my life hell.'

'All I was trying to do was make friends,' said Scarlett. 'You fell out with Farrah. You can't put that on me.'

'But you invited Farrah round for that weird sleepover,' I said. 'Way before me and Farrah fell out.'

'I didn't invite her,' said Scarlett. 'My stepdad did. I thought it was weird too, if you must know.'

'Why would your stepdad invite Farrah to a sleepover?' I asked.

'Because he's an idiot,' said Scarlett. 'And he didn't understand that sleepovers are for close friends. Is that why you did all that mean stuff at your party? Because I had Farrah for a sleepover?'

'What mean stuff?' I asked.

'Not telling me about the dress code,' said Scarlett. 'And giving everyone else a cowboy hat, except me. And not even *caring* when I was crying.'

I swallowed. Scarlett was right. I hadn't told her about the dress code. And I hadn't got her a cowboy hat. And I didn't try to make her feel better when she cried.

'And the name cards,' Scarlett continued. 'You drew little hearts on everyone's card, except mine.'

'I didn't know you,' I said. 'It would have been weird to draw hearts on your card. That's such a small thing, Scarlett. Do you really care about that?'

Small things add up,' said Scarlett. 'And FYI, attacking me at my birthday party wasn't a small thing.'

'Because you took that photograph,' I said. 'And then you made Farrah pull my hair on the way to school.'

'I didn't make her,' said Scarlett. 'And at least she didn't pull your hair *right out*.' She lifted her hair to show a bald spot.

We were both silent for a moment. Then Scarlett burst out laughing.

'What's so funny?' I said.

'We sound like idiots,' said Scarlett. 'We're both as bad as each other.'

'We both did bad things,' I said. 'But you did sneaky things on purpose.'

'Oh really?' said Scarlett. 'So you didn't throw a party on the same day as mine on purpose?'

'Okay,' I admitted. 'Yes. I did do that. But you were trying to steal my friends –'

'I was the new girl,' said Scarlett. 'I was just trying to meet people. And you felt threatened.'

'Does Scarlett have a point there, Lottie?' said Mrs Singh. 'Did you feel threatened?'

I sighed. 'Alright, yes. I suppose that's fair. I did feel threatened. I thought Scarlett was trying to steal my friends. But my sister says you can't steal real friends. She thinks Farrah and those girls were never my friends to begin with.'

'Do you know something?' said Scarlett. 'I don't think Farrah is my true friend either. She wouldn't give me the time of day if I didn't live in a big house.' She gave me kind eyes. 'Maybe we've both been played. When you think about it that way, we're on the same side.'

We both looked at each other, and something like understanding passed between us.

I turned to Mrs Singh. 'How come you didn't bring Farrah in here, too?'

'Because I agree with Scarlett,' said Mrs Singh. 'I think Farrah has been causing trouble. And I didn't want her buzzing around, confusing things. You two are the key to solving this problem. As soon as you start understanding each other, the other girls can't make drama. And then everyone will get along.'

'I can't really see Scarlett and me getting along,' I said. 'We're so different.'

'You're actually very similar,' said Mrs Singh. 'You're both strong people who know your own minds. The other girls look up to you. And you share a common interest.'

'Which is?' I asked.

'Dance,' said Mrs Singh. 'And with that in mind, I've had a rather clever idea.' She gave a flicker of a smile. 'Miss Miel and I have decided to put you *both* forward for the Dolores Rush Dance Contest.'

I stared at Mrs Singh. 'Both of us? How is that going to work? I withdrew my application and Scarlett has my dance squad. None of those girls will dance with me right now. And I don't want to dance with them either.'

'We've decided to enter you and Scarlett as a double act,' said Mrs Singh. 'Miss Miel checked the rules. A squad can comprise of two dancers. The rule is meant to cover sickness and absence but ... well, it's in there.'

'But what about Farrah, Primrose and Sophie?' asked Scarlett.

'Those girls won't be entering this year,' said Mrs Singh. 'It's just the two of you.'

'No way,' said Scarlett. 'No way can we dance together. We'll end up killing each other.'

'And Farrah will be furious,' I said. 'She'll go straight home to her parents and tell them you're being totally unfair.'

'Her parents can talk to me if there's an issue,' said Mrs Singh. 'Personally, I see it as a very fair punishment for those girls.'

'So, will Scarlett and I be punished too?' I asked.

'Well, I *am* making the two of you dance together,' said Mrs Singh.

Scarlett gave a little laugh.

'But Scarlett and I have never danced together,' I said. 'Don't you want our school to be in with a chance of winning? The contest is only a few weeks away. We can't come up with a two-person routine and practise it in that time.'

'I know it's short notice,' said Mrs Singh. 'But I'm sure your existing routines can be adapted. And Miss Miel has given me the key to the dance studio. She says you can have the studio all to yourselves before and after school and during PE lessons. You have double PE this morning, don't you?'

We both nodded.

Mrs Singh handed us a key with a pink ribbon on it. 'Here you are, girls. Guard it with your lives. Now, off you go. Do us proud.'

'How can we do you proud?' I asked. 'There's no way we'll win.'

Mrs Singh smiled. 'Maybe you'll win something better than a trophy.'

SCARLETT

It was a totally stupid idea.

Lottie and I pairing up for the Dolores Rush Dance Contest.

Don't get me wrong – I was happy Lottie and I talked it out. And I liked her a lot more once I'd understood her side of things. But dancing *together*?

Lottie is the most rigid, organised person I've ever met. Her dances are just technical steps to score points. They're so boring. No pizzazz or excitement. And I guess from Lottie's point of view, my routines are crazy.

Lottie and I walked out of Mrs Singh's office, sort of in shock. Our class had gone to their first lesson already, so it was weirdly quiet and empty.

'Well, that was unexpected,' I said.

'Yes,' said Lottie. 'Very much so.'

'At least we're in the contest,' I said. 'Even if we don't stand much chance of winning –'

'We have no chance of winning,' said Lottie. 'None.'

'There's always a chance,' I said. 'If we work really, really hard –'

'Look, I know you're desperate to win the scholarship,' said Lottie. 'Farrah told me you're having problems at home and want to move to London. I'm really sorry to hear that. Honestly I am. But you shouldn't get your hopes up. We're not going to win.'

I felt embarrassed then.

'You're being really negative,' I said. 'We're both dedicated. More dedicated than Farrah, Primrose and Sophie. Impossible is a state of mind. Right? We can do this.'

'I think we're just going to embarrass ourselves,' said Lottie.

'Oh, so what?' I said. 'At least we can say we tried.' I hesitated. 'Who's going to tell Farrah and those girls about the contest? Me or you?'

'Definitely you,' said Lottie. 'You're such great friends with them now. You get the honour of delivering the bad news.'

Lottie and I danced all morning, and it wasn't so bad. Okay, so Lottie and I didn't like each other. But we definitely respected each other. I thought Lottie was a great dancer, and I'm pretty sure she thought the same about me.

At break time, Farrah, Primrose and Sophie came to the dance studio.

Farrah looked totally shocked to see me and Lottie dancing together.

'What's going on?' she demanded.

'Miss Miel is entering us for the dance contest as a pair,' I explained. 'And she's given us exclusive use of the dance studio to practise.'

Farrah looked really annoyed. 'No way. She can't do that. What about us?'

'It's already done,' said Lottie. 'Miss Miel is filling out the entry form as we speak.'

'I'm going to complain to my parents,' said Farrah. 'Miss Miel can't do this. We've been practising for months. Haven't we, girls?'

She turned to Primrose and Sophie. They both looked at their feet.

'Miss Miel can choose whoever she wants for the dance contest,' I said. 'It's not like an exam or anything. This is extracurricular stuff.'

'But why should we miss out?' said Farrah. 'We didn't do anything wrong.'

'Mrs Singh knows about the bikini thing,' I said. 'She said it was a serious assault. And threatening to put the picture on WhatsApp ... Mrs Singh said I could go to prison for something like that.'

'Oh my god.' Farrah turned white. 'We were just joking.'

'It wasn't a joke,' I said. 'We were being mean and we took things too far. And I for one am really sorry. Lottie felt bullied. There are four of us and one of her.'

Sophie gasped. 'We're not *bullies*.'

'Look, we don't have time to talk about this right now,' I said. 'Lottie and I need to practise. A lot.'

Farrah huffed around for a while, and then she said: 'Well, you're not going to win the contest. So don't let it go to your head.'

After break time, we had science class. We had to look at honey under a microscope and write a report.

I sat with Farrah, which felt sort of weird. I'd been with Lottie all morning and it was like I was being two-faced, or something. After the conversation with Mrs Singh and seeing Lottie in tears like that ... well, I was beginning to see Farrah differently.

Lottie sat with Amina. I envied her. Amina is so friendly and straightforward.

When I sat down, Farrah asked, 'Did Lottie talk about me?'

'No,' I said. 'We were more focused on our dance routine.'

'Oh my god, Lottie is SO bossy,' said Farrah. 'I bet she was a nightmare to dance with, right? Like, worse than Hitler.' She blinked her big, blue eyes.

'Lottie definitely had opinions,' I said. 'But so did I. Actually, we worked pretty well together.'

Farrah snorted. 'Don't fall for it, Scarlett. Lottie's just putting on an act because she wants to win the competition.'

'I don't think so,' I said. 'She was really upset in Mrs Singh's office. I had no idea how much we were affecting her. Lottie has a vulnerable side. She just never shows it.'

'Lottie is about as vulnerable as a tiger,' said Farrah.

I could see I wasn't getting through to Farrah, so I didn't say anything else.

During the science lesson, Farrah kept making jokes

about Lottie. It was sort of mean, and I began to really wish I was in Amina and Lottie's group.

Towards the end of the lesson, Farrah said, 'Hey, look at Swotty Lottie, beavering away. She thinks she's so perfect. Let's pour this jar of honey into her school bag when she's not looking.'

Yesterday, I might have thought that would be funny. But now I'd seen Lottie in tears and we'd spent the morning dancing together ... well, it didn't seem so funny anymore.

'Cover for me,' said Farrah. 'I'm going in.'

'Let's just get on with our project,' I said.

'What's wrong with you?' said Farrah. 'Don't tell me you're turning into a nerd, like Lottie. I thought you were fun.' She snatched the jar of honey.

'Don't,' I said, grabbing her arm. 'Stop it, Farrah.'

'Stop what?'

'You know what,' I said.

Farrah sat back down and gave this really fake laugh.

'No need to take everything so seriously, Scarlett. I was just joking.'

LOTTIE

The next day, I thought about calling for Scarlett on my way to school. We'd both agreed to start school early for dance practice, but I couldn't quite bring myself to knock on Scarlett's door.

Scarlett and I were better, but not good. And I still felt upset about losing all my friends.

When I walked out onto the street, I found Scarlett waiting halfway between our houses.

'I thought I'd wait on the middle ground,' said Scarlett. 'Like no man's land in the war.'

'Why didn't you just knock on my door?' I asked.

'Why didn't you knock on my door?' Scarlett countered.

I shrugged. 'I don't know. I suppose I didn't want you to feel like you'd won.'

Scarlett rolled her eyes. 'Is everything about winning for you?'

'Winning and losing is a fact of life,' I said. 'You don't want to be a loser any more than I do.'

'Actually, I think experience is more important than winning,' said Scarlett.

'Yeah, right,' I said. 'So you're telling me you don't want to win this dance contest?'

'That's different,' said Scarlett. 'If I win this contest, my life will change forever.'

'Okay,' I said. 'So we're both in agreement. Winning is important.'

Scarlett laughed. 'Stop putting words into my mouth. Okay, fine. If it makes you feel better, I do want to win this dance contest. And so do you.'

'Yes,' I said. 'I do.'

'So we need to work harder to get along,' said Scarlett.

'That might be a tall order,' I said.

'Maybe,' said Scarlett. 'But we'll never know unless we try.' She reached out her hand. 'Why don't we agree to start afresh? Okay? I'll call for you tomorrow. We'll take it in turns.'

I hesitated. Part of me was beginning to like Scarlett. She actually seemed like a nice girl. And people hardly ever stand up to me. I respected her for that.

'Okay, fine.' I shook Scarlett's hand. 'And there's no need to take it in turns. I'll just call for you every day this week and next. You're on the way.'

We walked to school in silence for a while. A long while. Then Scarlett said, 'We did good work yesterday.'

'Yes.' I pulled a navy notepad from my bag. 'But we've got a lot more to do. I was working on ideas all last night. And I think we need to use at least three complicated ballet moves. And we need a story. That's a big thing in dance contests. If we can link the dance to something we're doing at school ... like Shakespeare or ... um ... Pythagoras triangles.'

'Pythagoras triangles?' said Scarlett. 'You want to do a dance based on Pythagoras triangles?'

'Why not?' I said. 'It shows we can combine ideas from the curriculum with our dance.'

'You're a really good dancer,' said Scarlett. 'But maybe you're a little too perfect. I entered lots of dance contests in New York and –'

'Did you win any?' I asked.

'No,' Scarlett admitted. 'But I saw a lot of winning entries. They always had something interesting about them. Perfect is boring.'

I glared at Scarlett. 'Are you calling my dance routines boring?'

'They are a little,' Scarlett laughed. 'I think people are scared to tell you the truth.'

'Well, your routines are all over the place,' I said. 'You never do the same thing twice. Dolores Rush will be watching for patterns and precision. If we don't do that, we'll lose points.'

'Do you know what I've been thinking about?' said Scarlett. 'Costumes. That's important too. We need to stand out.'

'We can't decide on costumes until we work out a story for our dance,' I said. 'You're trying to rush –'

'I have a story,' said Scarlett. 'Why don't we make our dance about bees? We're studying them in science. And you wanted something from the curriculum. There's a really cool piece of music ... 'The Flight of the Bumblebee' –'

'You want to do a bumblebee dance?' I said. 'Like we're four years old? What will we wear? Springy bee antennae on our foreheads?'

'No,' said Scarlett. 'We'll wear cool black and neon-yellow leotards. Big kohl eyes. Lots of black diamante on our faces. It'll be awesome. We'll really stand out. Look, I'll show you.'

Scarlett grabbed my notepad and pen and started scribbling amazing pictures.

'They look good,' I conceded. 'And we could make some of the moves look like real bees dancing. To show applied learning.'

'Do you know what?' said Scarlett. 'Maybe together, we'll come up with something better than either of us could have done alone. And blow this competition wide open. Stranger things have happened, right? Do you watch Stranger Things?'

'All the time,' I said.

'Not me,' said Scarlett. 'I find it way too scary.'

'Don't tell Farrah,' I said. 'She'll tease you for being a baby.'

We both laughed.

SCARLETT

It was so weird.

Lottie and I danced together for two weeks straight. At first, we argued more than we agreed. Then we agreed more than we argued. By week two, we actually began having fun together. We cheered each other on while we danced. And we talked – not just about dancing, but all sorts of things. Music, movies, fashion. Friends. Everything.

I spent so much time dancing with Lottie that I didn't have time for Farrah, Primrose and Sophie. And to be honest, I didn't miss them. Lottie, for all her faults, was a real person. She was spiky and bossy sometimes, but she didn't hide herself. Those other girls – they were just fake. I mean, how could they drop Lottie like that at the first sign of trouble?

By the end of the second week, something amazing happened. I started to like Lottie. I even gave her my phone number, and we talked about meeting up at the pizza park after the contest was over.

And the craziest thing of all? We honestly had a great dance routine. It was terrific. Dynamite. Boom! Better than anything I could have done on my own, and we did it in two weeks. Just incredible.

The Friday afternoon before the dance contest, Lottie and I walked home from school together.

'I'm so nervous about the contest,' said Lottie. 'Aren't you?'

'Totally,' I said. 'But we've got a fantastic routine. We've worked every free moment for the past two weeks. The only thing to do now is rest up for tomorrow.'

'No way,' said Lottie. 'We can't rest. We're not polished enough. Dolores Rush looks for precision and flair. We have the flair. But every step needs to be perfect. We should go over and over everything as much as possible.'

'How?' I asked. 'School is closed up for the weekend. We gave the dance studio key back to Mrs Singh.'

'We could always practise at my house,' said Lottie. 'I

mean, I know it's teeny tiny compared to your great big mansion ...'

We both laughed.

'My house definitely has space for us to dance,' I said. 'You can come over if you promise not to beat me up.'

Lottie looked guilty for a moment, but when she saw my playful expression she burst out laughing.

So that's how Lottie ended up at my house on the Friday before the dance contest.

'I never thought you'd invite me back here,' said Lottie, as we headed out to the garden. 'To the scene of the crime.'

'Me either,' I said. 'Don't start any trouble. Zara isn't here to pull you off this time.'

'What about your mother?' Lottie asked. 'Is she home?'

'Mum always works late,' I said. 'She's never home before eight o'clock. Some nights, she's not back until I've gone to bed.'

'What about your stepfather?' Lottie asked.

'He's either in his office working or in London,' I said. 'We usually stay out of each other's way.'

'So you're all alone?' Lottie asked, looking around the garden. 'In this great big house?'

I nodded.

'You must hate that,' I said. 'You're a people person.'

'I do hate it,' I said. 'But if I win the scholarship, I can live in London near my sister and dance all day. It's basically my dream come true.'

'Wow,' said Lottie. 'That's so weird.'

'What?' I asked.

'Everyone in the village envies your big house,' said Lottie. 'They all think you're so lucky. But you want to get out of it.'

I shrugged. 'It's people that make you happy, not things.

I'd rather be in a dorm full of girls than a big house, all alone.'

'That makes sense,' said Lottie. 'I'd hate to be in a dorm, though. Ugh. I'm really bad at sharing my space.'

'So why are *you* entering the contest, Lottie?' I asked. 'Don't *you* want a place at a dance academy in London?'

'No way,' said Lottie. 'If I won, I'd use the cash prize to pay for my university fees. All I want to do is prove I'm the best dancer.' She hesitated. 'You'd really move to London?'

'In a heartbeat,' I said. 'I'd love to board with other girls and I could see Zara at the weekends. For the first time in my life, I'd have a family.'

'But you already have a family,' said Lottie.

'No I don't.' I said. 'Not like you do.'

Lottie sighed. 'You know, my family looks good on the outside, but my parents argue all the time. Mum is always keeping secrets from Dad and ... well, sometimes I think they might split up.'

'Sorry,' I said. 'I didn't know that.'

'No one does,' said Lottie. 'You're the first person I've told.'

'I won't tell anyone,' I said.

'I know.' Lottie nodded. 'You're not like Farrah and those girls.'

We smiled at each other.

'Are we becoming friends now?' I asked.

Lottie laughed. 'Maybe.'

'Are you still feeling nervous about the contest?' I asked.

'Terrified,' said Lottie. 'I know we've got a good routine, but I keep landing steps wrong and forgetting to smile. I let my middle sag all the time –'

'What are you talking about?' I said. 'You're an amazing

dancer. Look, I know you're Little Miss Perfect, but you're being really hard on yourself.'

'I'm far from perfect,' said Lottie. 'I'm the shortest girl in our class, I'm rubbish at maths and I wear glasses. I just try really, really hard, because winning is so important in my family.'

'I like your glasses,' I said. 'You look sort of clever and pretty at the same time.'

'So how come you and Farrah were laughing about them behind my back?' said Lottie.

I felt embarrassed then. 'Look, I'm sorry about that,' I said. 'Actually, we weren't laughing about your glasses. We were laughing about you being so angry. It just looked sort of silly.'

'You called me an angry librarian,' said Lottie. 'I heard.'

'I didn't,' I said. 'Farrah said that.'

'Oh.' Lottie nodded. 'I thought it was you.'

'I did laugh along though,' I admitted. 'Sorry.'

'It's okay,' said Lottie. 'I'm really sorry I attacked you.' Then she gave me serious eyes. 'Honestly. I really am truly sorry. I was just so angry and jealous.'

'It's okay,' I said. 'I took that photo thing way too far. I honestly didn't know Farrah was going to mess with your bikini when I took the picture. It was bad timing. But I never should have joked around like that. I should have just deleted the photo right away.'

We smiled at each other, and they were genuine smiles.

On the outside, Lottie has this hard shell. She seems arrogant and rude and unfriendly, and she can be all those things. But there's a reason. Underneath it all, she's as scared as the rest of us.

LOTTIE

The dance contest came around way too quickly.

Honestly.

I felt like I blinked and two weeks passed. Scarlett and I had been practising non-stop, but we just weren't ready.

On the morning of the contest, I was a total bundle of nerves.

When Scarlett turned up at my house, I was practically shaking.

'We haven't practised enough,' I gabbled. 'We haven't even had a dress rehearsal.'

Scarlett laughed and held up two bags of black and yellow fabric. 'How could we? I only finished our costumes last night.'

'Why don't we do a dress rehearsal now?' I asked.

'Because your mum is waiting in the car,' said Scarlett. 'And she just sounded her horn. I think she's as nervous as you are. We've practised enough, Lottie. Honestly. Our routine is fantastic.'

But I didn't feel that way. I mean ... no *dress* rehearsal?

Oh my god.

On the drive to London, Mum stressed me out even more.

'Remember, the standards here are very high,' said Mum. 'You can't afford to lose a second of concentration. Keep your stomachs tight and your chins up. And make sure you check your makeup just before you go on stage. Nerves make you sweat and your makeup can smudge. Oh, and use a towel for the sweat. I packed one for each of you. And above all, remember to smile, smile, smile.'

It went on and on.

I looked at Scarlett and rolled my eyes. Scarlett tried not to laugh.

Finally, we arrived at the dance academy and Mum was taken to the audience area with the other parents.

'Thank goodness Mum's gone,' I told Scarlett, as we entered the huge changing room. 'She was freaking me out.'

'She's just nervous,' said Scarlett. 'At least she cares.'

'Oh my god!' I grabbed Scarlett's arm. 'Look at those ballet tutus. I bet they cost a fortune. The diamanté alone ... so much work.'

'They're beautiful,' Scarlett agreed. 'But you haven't seen ours yet.'

Scarlett opened her bags and took out two bright yellow catsuits with sparkling black stripes.

'You're kidding me.' I stared at the costumes. 'I can't wear that. It's way too much. I mean ... those outfits are so *yellow*. They could stop traffic. And they're *catsuits*.'

'The idea is to stand out,' said Scarlett. 'Ordinary isn't good enough when there are hundreds of other entries. We need to go bright and bold or go home.'

'Well, we've certainly gone bright,' I said. 'These costumes are from a different planet.'

'Exactly,' said Scarlett. 'That's the whole point. Who's going to notice one more girl in a pretty leotard? Now about your hair ...'

'What about it?' I touched my neat, brown bun.

'It needs neon,' said Scarlett, pulling spray cans from her bag. 'Yellow neon. Which I just happen to have brought.'

'I can't wear *fluorescent* yellow hair spray,' I cried. 'Please, Scarlett. It's just not me. I *can't*.'

'You can,' said Scarlett. 'And you will.'

Scarlett is the only person I've ever met who can tell me what to do like that.

'Maybe just a tiny bit at the back,' I said.

'You need LOTS,' said Scarlett, shaking up a can of yellow. 'Trust me. On stage, everything has to be ten times as obvious. Oh, and you need to funk up your glasses too.' Scarlett pulled out a bag full of glittery black crystal stickers. 'We'll stick these around the frame to make them really cool.'

'No way,' I said. 'I don't want to draw attention to my glasses.'

'Yes you do,' said Scarlett. 'There are hundreds of dancers here, but I haven't seen anyone else in glasses. If we make your glasses stand out, we'll be totally one of a kind.'

'Okay fine.' I gave a nervous nod, knowing Scarlett was probably right. 'Just do it.'

By the time Scarlett had finished with my hair and makeup, I looked REALLY dynamic. I mean, I stood OUT. There was no missing me. And my glasses looked great. A lot less like boring old man glasses. I wished I'd stuck things on the frames ages ago.

Also, when Scarlett and I went to queue backstage, people told me how cool my glasses were. Which felt great.

'See?' Scarlett whispered. 'We're making everyone smile and we're not even on stage.'

'God, I'm nervous,' I whispered. 'Aren't you nervous?'

'A little,' said Scarlett. 'But it's more like excitement. We're getting to dance on this huge stage in front of all these people. What's the worst that can happen?'

'We get the moves wrong, make total fools of ourselves and don't win anything,' I said.

'So what?' said Scarlett. 'At least we tried.' She put an arm around my shoulder. 'Anyway, we've already won. Right?'

'How do you work that one out?' I asked.

'Because we're friends now. Mrs Singh was right. There are better things to win than trophies.'

SCARLETT

The dance contest was held at the Dolores Rush Dance Academy in London. It was the most amazing place I'd ever seen.

Wow.

A *school* dedicated to dancing.

My idea of heaven. And the whole place felt electric. There were so many kids, stretching and bouncing around, sharing dancing tips and wishing each other good luck. You could practically feel the energy through the floor.

Lottie's mother was a little overbearing. She kept going on and on about posture and makeup and that kind of thing. I felt sorry for Lottie. You could tell the advice was freaking her out.

It was a relief when Mrs Collins was led away to a parents' area, so Lottie and I could change alone backstage.

I thought Lottie might have a heart attack when she saw our costumes. For someone who likes to be the best at everything, Lottie doesn't enjoy standing out. Which is sort of crazy.

I told her, 'Standing out is the name of the game.'

It took a little persuading, but Lottie let me spray her hair yellow to go with our bright yellow outfits. I made over her glasses too, which looked awesome. Then we were called to wait by the stage.

'I'm going to be sick,' said Lottie, as we watched other acts perform. 'Honestly. I'm going to throw up. I've never been so underprepared in my life.'

'The waiting is the hardest part,' I told her. 'Once we get on stage, it'll be absolutely fine. You'll see.'

We kept moving up the line, and eventually, we were the next act to go on.

On stage, a group of energetic boys did backflips and spins. They had glowing letters on their chests and moved around to spell different things. It was really cool. Finally, they stood in a line and spelt TIME OUT, their squad name. The audience cheered and whooped.

'Oh my god,' said Lottie. 'They were so good. I don't think I can do this, Scarlett. I don't know my steps well enough. What if I forget everything and look totally stupid?'

I grabbed Lottie's hand and held it really tight. 'Lottie,' I said. 'We're both dressed in yellow and black striped catsuits. We already look stupid. Now let's go on stage and make everyone smile.'

I didn't give Lottie time to get more nervous. I just pulled her on stage.

There were a lot of people in the audience. Maybe a thousand. I gave Lottie a reassuring grin.

'Remember to have fun,' I told her. 'It's only three minutes. Right?'

I was still holding Lottie's hand when the music started – a really cool version of 'Flight of the Bumblebee'.

It was great actually, because the audience were already smiling before we'd even started dancing. It was such a funny mash-up of the song.

I started spinning around really fast. For a horrible moment, I thought Lottie wasn't going to move. Her face was totally white and tense. But then she did a perfect pirouette and got a round of applause. After that, she was great. Smiling and full of energy.

I did some really high leaps and landed my backflip, which felt awesome.

When we finished our routine, Lottie and I were laughing hysterically.

'We did it!' we said. 'We did it!'

The audience clapped and cheered. We definitely got their attention, although I didn't know if it was for the right reasons.

'Thank god that's over,' said Lottie, as we headed backstage.

I laughed. 'I could do it all over again.'

'Because you're a massive show off,' said Lottie, giving me a friendly pat on the arm.

'And you're totally bossy and full of yourself,' I told her.

Some of the other kids stared at us then. Like, why are they being rude to each other?

We didn't bother explaining. It was just one of those jokes between friends.

LOTTIE

Oh my god.

I was SO nervous. I totally froze on stage. Honestly, when I saw the size of the audience, I nearly had a heart attack. I kept thinking about Mum, telling me to suck in my stomach and keep my chin up.

Scarlett and I had worked so hard on our routine, but I still felt underprepared. I mean, I'd never, ever danced in a catsuit before.

When the music started, I just stood there, like an idiot.

Luckily, Scarlett started first. She was so joyful and relaxed. If she hadn't been there, I probably would have run off stage in tears. But I managed my first pirouette and everyone applauded. After that, things got easier. Not easy, but easier.

It was such a relief when we finished the dance. Scarlett and I kept high-fiving each other and squealing.

'We did it! We did it!'

Once we'd changed into our own clothes, we met Mum for snacks and drinks in the breakout area. There was fresh fruit, but only Scarlett ate that. Everyone else had chocolate chip cookies and crisps – me included.

'Why do you still have those stickers around your glasses, Lottie?' Mum asked me.

'Because they're fun,' I said.

Mum looked like she wanted to say something, but she didn't.

After the snack break, we all went into the auditorium for the prize giving. I felt nervous again, but I knew there was nothing else Scarlett and I could do. Win or lose, we'd done our best.

The auditorium fell silent as Dolores Rush came onto the stage.

I'd only ever seen Dolores on TV before, and she was much smaller in real life. Really tiny. It made me happy to think that a small person could be a famous dancer.

Dolores looked great for an older lady. Fit and toned, with gleaming black skin. She had very short, white hair, which was a surprise. On TV, she has flowing, brown hair with lots of beaded plaits, so I suppose she must wear hairpieces.

Dolores did a pirouette in her evening dress, before taking the microphone. Everyone clapped. Then the audience fell silent.

'Welcome to the fifth Dolores Rush Dance Contest, wonderful people.' Dolores smiled and surveyed the crowd.

'My word. The talent this year. Phew! I could barely catch my breath. Okay. Let's get started with the prizes.'

The younger children were called first, and after what seemed like forever, Dolores announced our age group.

'I was very, very impressed with you all,' said Dolores. 'And my goodness, it was hard to choose. But there can only be one winner. So without further ado, let me award the best tween and teen dance act to our all-boy dance group, Time Out. Well done, boys. Come up on stage and collect your prizes.'

'Oh, what a *shame*,' said Mum, as Time Out headed to the stage. 'You two should have won. You were brilliant. What were those judges thinking?'

Honestly. My mother can be so embarrassing sometimes.

Dolores gave Time Out their trophy and prize envelopes, then sent them back into the cheering audience.

'Now, we have our final prize.' Dolores gave us a dazzling smile. 'Awarded to the most outstanding solo dancer.'

There were whispers and murmurs in the audience.

'Solo prize?' said Mum. 'Could one of you girls win this, maybe?'

I shook my head. 'Solo prizes go to the best dancer within one of the winning squads. And we weren't a winning squad.'

'Oh, that's disappointing,' said Mum. 'Maybe next year.' She shifted to the edge of her seat. 'Let's be quiet now. She's announcing the prize.'

The audience fell silent.

'And so, our solo prize,' said Dolores. 'Awarded to our favourite dancer from the whole competition. A young person who had such joy and such passion. We believe this dancer has something very, very special and we hope will certainly take a scholarship at my school. The prize goes to ...' Dolores held up the trophy. 'Scarlett King from St Valentine's School.'

Scarlett and I stared at each other.

'No *way*,' Scarlett breathed.

I gave a scream of delight.

Scarlett clamped both hands over her mouth. 'Oh my god,' she said. 'Oh my god. There must be a mistake. We weren't a winning squad.'

'There's no mistake,' I said. 'Didn't you hear what they said about joy and passion? It's totally you.' My voice rose to a shriek. 'You won, Scarlett! You won!'

It was weird. I felt such joy and I hadn't won anything myself. It was a brand-new experience and a wonderful one.

'Your dream came true,' I squealed. 'You won the scholarship.'

Scarlett didn't move.

'Where's Scarlett?' asked Dolores, looking around the crowd.

'HERE!' I shouted.

'Lottie, I can't.' Scarlett gave me urgent eyes. 'This isn't real. It must be a mistake. Things like this don't happen to me. Maybe Dolores read the wrong name –'

'Go and accept your future.' I pulled Scarlett to her feet. 'If you don't walk, I'll drag you up there.'

'You couldn't lift me,' said Scarlett. 'You're too short.'

'I'm stronger than I look. Come *on*.'

I dragged Scarlett through the audience and towards the stage. She looked sort of dazed like she couldn't quite believe what was happening.

'You're in shock,' Dolores laughed, as I led Scarlett up the stage steps. 'Don't worry. We'll take good care of you.'

'Are you sure this isn't a mistake?' Scarlett asked Dolores. 'Our squad didn't win.'

'It was such a close contest this year,' said Dolores. 'Your squad came so close to winning. And you were our favourite dancer, Scarlett. Hands down.' Dolores turned to me and smiled. 'It's good to see your wonderful dance partner on stage too. We loved your glasses, young lady. And we hope to see you back next year.'

I nodded and smiled.

Dolores put a kind arm around Scarlett's shoulder.

'We were very, very impressed with your dancing, Scarlett,' she said. 'You really put your heart and soul into your performance. Here is your prize, darling. A scholarship to my school, and a cheque for £100,000.'

Scarlett burst into tears.

Everyone clapped and cheered, but I clapped the loudest.

I was so happy for Scarlett. Seeing my friend win such an important contest ... well, it was amazing. So much better than winning myself.

It turned out Mrs Singh was right. I won something much better than a trophy.

My prize was a new friend.

SCARLETT

I couldn't believe it.

One minute, I was sitting in the dance contest audience, clapping for all the other prize winners. The next, I was on stage, crying like an idiot.

Dolores was so warm and kind. She gave me a big hug and told me I was something very special.

As I took my medal and golden envelope, Lottie clapped harder than anyone.

'Go Scarlett!' she cheered. 'Whoop whoop!'

When we went back to our seats, Lottie's mum gave me a handshake. 'Well done, Scarlett. I'm happy you got that scholarship. I know how much you wanted it.'

'I wish Lottie could have won a prize too,' I said. 'She worked just as hard. Lottie, you should take the prize money. And I'll take the scholarship.'

'No way.' Lottie shook her head. 'You won fair and square. And you heard what Dolores said. There's always next year.'

'Well, take the trophy at least,' I said.

'*No.*' Lottie gave me fierce eyes. 'You won it. It's yours. Anyway, what do I need another trophy for? I have so many.'

We both laughed.

'Just promise me one thing,' said Lottie. 'You'll get me front row tickets for your first West End show.'

'Deal,' I said.

'So when will you take up this scholarship, Scarlett?' said Mrs Collins. 'After the summer holidays?'

'I guess so.'

'I'll miss you so much,' said Lottie.

'I'll miss you too,' I said.

Who'd have thought two girls who hated each other could become such good friends?

Things changed at St Valentine's after the dance competition.

Lottie and I hung out a lot, but we didn't dance together at break times. Instead, Lottie wrote stories and played word games with Amina and Marianne. It was much more Lottie's sort of thing, and once she stopped caring about looking swotty or being a baby, she was happy.

I still danced at break times, but with older girls. I didn't want to hang out with Farrah, Primrose and Sophie anymore. Once I heard Lottie's side of things ... well. If those girls could turn on Lottie like that, I didn't want to know them. I wanted real friends, not fake ones.

For a while, Farrah told the teachers that Lottie and I were bullying her.

'They're leaving me out,' she said. 'They're being so mean.'

We kept explaining that we weren't leaving Farrah out. We just didn't want to hang around with her anymore. The teachers thought that was fair enough.

Then Primrose and Sophie had a big falling out over a boy. They each found new friendship groups and spread rumours about each other. It was pretty sad.

Eventually, Farrah moved to another school. Her parents said there was a bullying problem at St Valentine's. Which was sort of funny, because Farrah was definitely part of the bullying problem.

After the summer holidays, I joined the Dolores Rush Dance Academy. I've been here for nearly four months now, and it's everything I dreamed of and more.

Dolores is such a big-hearted, warm person and her school feels like home. I've made some amazing friends already, and we have so much fun together.

Yes, there are one or two difficult characters. But after my time at St Valentine's, I know how to keep everyone in line. We're like one big family here, and we look after each other.

Sometimes, Lottie, Amina and Marianne visit me at the

weekends, and we have fun girly sleepovers at Zara's apartment. I feel so lucky to have met them.

I still FaceTime my New York friends too, and some of them are coming to see me at Christmas.

Actually, I'm hoping my New York friends and Lottie, Amina and Marianne will all come down at the same time to see my show. That's right. I'm in a show. A big one. I'm dancing in Oliver at the Apollo Theatre, and I am SO excited.

Obviously, I'll get my friends front row seats. I have it all planned out. My friends will watch the show, then come backstage and meet the cast. After that, we'll go to this cool American diner place in Soho. They have awesome burgers and milkshakes. It'll be so much fun.

So this is my life right now. Dancing every day. Winning parts in musicals and on TV. Being around kind, big-hearted people. Having amazing friends.

I'm so happy.

The happiest I've ever been.

THANK YOU FOR READING

If you have a minute, please review.
I read all my Amazon and Goodreads reviews
(yes, the bad ones do make me cry) and good reviews mean everything.
Reviews don't have to be fancy. In fact, just one word is great (as long as it isn't 'rubbish' ...). And they do more good than you could ever imagine.

Suzy K Quinn xx

ABOUT THE AUTHOR

Suzy K Quinn writes romantic comedy, children's books, young adult and thrillers.

Her novels have been translated into ten languages and her books have sold over 750,000 copies worldwide.

She lives in Wivenhoe, Essex, with her husband Demi, two daughters, eight fish and a snail.

Email: contact@suzykquinn.com
Facebook.com/suzykquinn (Suzy still accepts friend requests.)
Twitter/TikTok: @suzykquinn
Website: suzykquinn.com

MORE BOOKS BY SUZY K QUINN

Magical Mystery for Children

Huxley Sparks and the Book of Secrets (Summer 2022)

School Drama for Children

Trouble Maker (Spring 2022)

Romantic Comedy for Adults

The Bad Mother Series

1. The Bad Mother's Diary
2. The Bad Mother's Detox
3. The Bad Mother's Holiday
4. The Bad Mother's Christmas
5. The Bad Mother's Virus
6. The Bad Mother's Wedding

Free Novella: The Bad Mother Begins (visit suzykquinn.com to download)

Printed in Great Britain
by Amazon

75588361R10104